Intermediate GNVQ Health and Social Care

Margaret Sanderson *and* Mike Williams

MACMILLAN

First published 1996 by
MACMILLAN PRESS LTD
Houndmills, Basingstoke, Hampshire RG21 6XS
and London
Companies and representatives
throughout the world

ISBN 0–333–61705–3

A catalogue record for this book is available
from the British Library

Designed by Susan Clarke
Typeset by 𝍐 Tek Art, Croydon, Surrey
Printed in Hong Kong

10   9   8   7   6   5   4   3   2   1
05   04   03   02   01   00   99   98   97   96

Contents

Preface

The aims of this book

This book has been written to support your work in the Intermediate level **General National Vocational Qualification (GNVQ) in Health and Social Care**. Its aim, as you start out on your education and training, is to give you a broad introduction to the knowledge and skills expected of a professional care worker, and an understanding of how these are achieved within the requirements and framework of a GNVQ programme.

Looked at individually, many of the duties and skills involved in care work may seem fairly straightforward and easy to perform: don't be misled by this. Caring for people is never a matter of repetitively applying the same routines and skills irrespective of the people and circumstances concerned. It is a highly complex job, in which each duty and responsibility can, and often does, involve a variety of different skills, abilities, knowledge, personal choices and decisions. That's what makes it a *professional* job.

This book is designed with these aims:

- to introduce you to GNVQs, and to help you to understand what they involve and how they work;
- to introduce you to the variety of roles and responsibilities performed by people working in the field of health and social care;
- to help you to understand and to develop the knowledge, skills and professional attitudes necessary for employment, or for further study and training, in health and social care;
- to help you to get the best out of your studies in order to gain an Intermediate GNVQ in Health and Social Care.

An integrated approach

The book has been written as an introduction to your studies, to be used alongside the guidance and support you will receive from your tutors in school or in college, and from the professionals you will meet in the workplace. The work covered in the book links very closely with the material in the GNVQ health and social care units; Units 2 and 4, for example, are the basis for the content of Chapters 4, 5 and 6 of the book, and Units 1 and 3 provide the basis for much of Chapter 7. In the same way, many of the tasks and activities you are asked to carry out are linked to the core skills units and provide you with opportunities to develop and demonstrate the core skills you require.

A key aim of the book, therefore, is to build up your understanding of how the knowledge, skills and professional attitudes involved in working as a carer come together in actually doing the job. This is sometimes referred to as an *integrated* approach to learning and training. The idea is to focus on the situation as you might find it in real life, and to look at what you need to know and to do in order to respond successfully to all the demands of that particular situation. Making sense of a situation or problem is always the first thing that a professional will be called upon to do, so you need to get used to this type of thinking and responsibility right from the start.

Caring is essentially a practical activity. In order to perform effectively in a practical situation it is not enough just to know *about* the information, skills and personal qualities you will need in that situation: you must also know *how* and *when* to use these. Caring is about working with people and making appropriate decisions and judgements in relation to their differing needs and circumstances. Knowing what action to take in such situations is not something that is easily taught: it needs to be learned over time.

This book doesn't give you ready-made answers to all the situations and issues you may meet as a carer: its purposes are to provide you with opportunities to see and examine for yourself what is involved in caring, to present you with examples of caring in action, and to help you to experience what it's like to think in a professional way about the issues and responsibilities that you may one day face.

Acknowledgements

The authors would like to thank all those who have helped during the preparation of this book: in particular their families and friends, for their sustained encouragement and support; Chris Brooker, for reading and reviewing the text; David Llewellyn, for his patience and advice on computers; Joy Hermite, for her contribution to the artwork; and Alison Heath, who read an early draft of the text.

The authors and publishers wish to thank the following for permission to use copyright material: Age Resource 1991 – Woodworking with the Retired and Senior Volunteer Programme, Isle of Wight – photograph page 56; Peter Hayman/Lynda King (Proprietor, Rose Cottage Residential Home, Broughton, Cambridgeshire) – photograph page 52; The Hulton Deutsch Collection – illustration page 78; Kensington and Chelsea College – photograph page 90; Norfolk College – photographs page 92; and NCVQ – grading criteria extracts page 27. The cover illustration is by John Birdsall Photography.

Every effort has been made to trace all copyright holders, but if any have been inadvertently overlooked the publishers will be pleased to make the necessary arrangement at the first opportunity.

Introduction

As you work through this book, you will probably be struck by how much there is to cover, how much there is to learn, and how many skills you will need to acquire in order to become a responsible and effective professional in health and social care.

Different starting-points . . .

Each of you will have your own needs and reasons for using this book, and these are likely to differ from other people's needs and reasons. You will be approaching it from a variety of different *starting-points*. Some of you may have already studied for a GNVQ, while others of you may have experience of working as a care worker. Alternatively, some of you may still be uncertain about your choice of future career and the courses available to you, and be using this book to help you to make up your mind.

. . . Same finishing-point

Whatever your starting-point, by the time that you complete a GNVQ in Health and Social Care, whether at school or college, each of you will have reached a common *finishing-point*. The things that marked out you and your colleagues as different at the beginning of the course will have become less evident and less important. You will all need to have reached a defined standard of work and achievement in order to be awarded the GNVQ. This is a fixed standard for all students for the award.

Starting out on a GNVQ in Health and Social Care

A PRACTICAL WORKBOOK

The material is presented in a practical way, for you to use in a variety of ways. It can be used, for instance, as a personal guide and introduction to your studies; as a source of factual information and knowledge; as a starting-point for personal and group discussions; or for developing and testing your learning through practical activities and tasks. Ideally, it will serve all these purposes.

Learning how to learn

Whatever its purpose for you, the book is designed to help you to learn. To get the best out of the book, therefore, you will have to do your share of the work! Why? Because studying for a qualification in health and social care is not about being given the answers by tutors and books; it is about learning how to respond to the practical circumstances, needs and issues presented by real people in a real world. This means accepting some of the responsibility for your own learning. As a carer you will assume responsibility for other people's lives in all sorts of ways. Understanding what taking personal responsibility feels like, and what it involves, is an important aspect of your training.

There is another reason for this approach. As we observed earlier, working successfully with people is not something that can be taught; it's something you learn through practice as well as through acquiring knowledge from books. A distinction was made between knowing *about* something and knowing *how* or *when* to do something. Knowing how and when to take action is a form of knowledge that takes time to develop and acquire. It is important to understand the distinction between these two types of knowledge. We call one **theory** and the other **practice**, or **practical knowledge**.

Theory and practice

The best way to gain practical knowledge is through practice, that is, *learning through doing*. In contrast, information learnt from a book, or from what someone has told you, is theory: it only becomes practical knowledge when you make use of the theory to carry out an actual task.

The difference can be seen if we take as an example learning to ride a bicycle. In principle you could get the information you need from a book. You could then claim to know about how it's done – in *theory*. But this wouldn't mean that you knew how to do it in *practice*. Most people learn to ride a bike by having a go. Through trial and error and a few bruises, they find out how it is actually done. This is practical knowledge. You cannot learn to ride a bike from theory alone.

A word of warning, though. Practical knowledge is not all that you ever need. The professional responsibilities and duties you will be required to carry out as a care worker are very different from the largely repetitive and unthinking activity of riding a bike. Caring involves *people*. Using a trial-and-error approach with people's lives is not acceptable. Imagine, for example, that you have to respond to a situation in which it is your responsibility to make the arrangements for the care of an elderly woman whose husband has just been admitted to hospital as an emergency. How would you feel about taking on this responsibility, in terms of the trust that it places in your knowledge and skill?

- Would you be happy just to 'have a go' at it?
- How do you think the elderly woman would feel if this were your approach?

The message is clear. Working in health and social care requires that you have a high level of *both* theoretical *and* practical knowledge. One thing more is needed if you are to feel confident about the decisions you reach, and that is **experience**. And that comes from practice.

What the book covers

Chapter 1 is a guide to the GNVQ as a framework for your course of study. This chapter helps you to become familiar at an early stage in your studies with many of the words and terms that are used throughout the book. It also takes a stage further the theme of giving you responsibility for much of your own learning. If you require basic information about health and social care and about GNVQs you will need to read the early sections of this chapter carefully.

Chapter 2 takes the general information about GNVQs and the introductory description of health and social care and combines them into an outline of the content of the GNVQ in Health and Social Care at Intermediate level. It also introduces you to some of the skills and ways of thinking that you will need to develop in order to be a professional carer, and to take responsibility for your own learning.

Chapter 3 builds upon this information and introduces you to how you are assessed, and what is needed to gain the GNVQ award. *Grading criteria* and *action plans* are introduced through a series of activities and tasks for you to carry out. The ways in which your work is assessed are described, and practical advice is given on how to present your work. Chapters 2 and 3 are a source of information and reference, to be used throughout your studies as needed.

Chapter 4 continues with the theme of making you an active participant in your own learning. The chapter aims to help you understand the complexity of people as individuals and groups, and the reasons why they are complex. This is done by first looking at you as an individual and exploring some of the factors and circumstances that make you the person *you* are. At the end of the chapter you are introduced to an imaginary situation in the form of a story about a group of people living in a street on the edge of a large town. The story provides the basis for the work and activities covered in Chapters 5, 6 and 7.

Chapters 5 and 6 take the people in the story, and the issues that surround them, and relate these to the duties and responsibilities of the care worker and to the work of the health and care services. This involves looking at, and understanding, the lives of other people. Chapter 5 uses the older people in the story as a focus for some of the general skills and understanding you need to acquire and develop. Chapter 6 then explores the needs of a young family in the story. These circumstances raise a variety of issues about the role of the family in shaping our individuality, and about the role of the community in providing the focus for the organisation and operation of the health and care services locally. (Chapters 4, 5 and 6 are closely linked to the requirements of Units 2 and 4 of the GNVQ.)

Chapter 7 outlines the structure of the health and care services. It describes the services that are available and the ways in which people can make use of these. Again, the focus is the community. The chapter also includes an introduction to your responsibilities as a health promoter. Lastly, it looks at you, the carer, and the demands made upon you in terms of your own well-being. (Chapter 7 relates to Units 1 and 3 of the GNVQ.)

Finally, Chapter 8 looks at the range of services provided by the library and how best to make use of them. Lists are also given of the names and addresses of key agencies and organisations in health and social care which might be useful to you. Chapter 8 also provides a list of further reading related to the various topics covered in the book. Lastly, it reminds you how important it is to make full use of the help and support available to you. This chapter should be read and consulted at the beginning of your course, and throughout it, as required.

Key words and technical terms

You will sometimes come across technical terms which may not be familiar to you, or words that have different meanings when used in relation to health and social care. Many of these words and terms are identified and explained in the text. Lists of key words and technical terms with definitions are also given, so that you can check their meaning. Knowing and using the correct words and terms is an important part of being professional. Also, keep a dictionary to hand, so that you can check any words which are not explained in the text.

GETTING ON THE RIGHT PROGRAMME

The rest of this chapter will help you find out about GNVQ courses in health and social care. It is aimed at readers who are still unsure about what is involved in applying for a course in health and social care, and how to get the information they need. If you have already started your course, or studied for a GNVQ before, you can omit these sections.

First questions

These are likely to begin with the words *what* or *where*:

- What is health and social care?
- What is a GNVQ?
- What opportunities does the GNVQ in Health and Social Care offer me?
- What does studying for the GNVQ in Health and Social Care involve?
- Where can I study for the GNVQ?
- Where can I find out about the GNVQ in my local area?

Finding out

If you want details about courses on offer in health and social care, contact your local careers office, further education (FE) college, or sixth-form centre. If you're not sure where they are, look them up in the telephone directory for the address and phone number, or ask at a library. If you are at school the careers officer or teacher will have information about GNVQs.

Making contact

It is a good idea to make contact with the local FE college or sixth-form centre yourself either by writing and asking for information or by telephoning and asking for an appointment with a member of staff who can discuss the GNVQ in Health and Social Care with you.

Applying

If you are asked to fill in an **application form**, use it as an opportunity to give as much information about yourself as possible. If, for instance, you help your grandparents, or you babysit for a neighbour or a relative, or have an interest in a particular voluntary group, include this information on the form so that your involvement with people can be discussed when you go for the interview.

If you are invited to attend an interview, try to visit the college or centre beforehand to look around the facilities there for students.

Interview

Before an **interview**, spend some time thinking about what you need to know. An interview is as much a chance for you to find out what you need to know as for others to assess your suitability for a course of study.

You might want answers to the following questions:

- How long will the Intermediate GNVQ in Health and Social Care take to complete?
- Would I have to attend college or school every day?
- What subjects would I study?
- What opportunities exist at the end of the course for further study, or employment?
- Would I have to pay towards the cost of the course?
- Would I be eligible to apply for a grant?
- Is it possible to claim for assistance towards the costs of travel and books?

There may also be questions that you need to ask yourself:

- What would I have to give up in order to fit the course into my life?
- Am I really committed to studying full-time?
- Would it be better if I studied as a part-time student?

Only you can answer these questions.

Asking around

If possible, speak to students already enrolled on the GNVQ in Health and Social Care to find out from them what it is like. If, after all this, you are still undecided on the best course of action for you, arrange to discuss your future with someone from the **careers service**. Don't make a decision until you are absolutely sure that a particular course is right for you.

Induction

If you are new to a school or college, the course is likely to begin with a short settling-in period designed to introduce you to the programme and to the college or school. This is called **induction**. It may last two or three days, depending on what is covered. It is an important time for you because it gives you the chance to get to know the college or school in which you are studying, to get to know what is involved in your programme of study and, most importantly, to get to know other students.

Here are two tasks which might be included in an induction programme, designed to help you to develop a good working relationship with others. The first one is about finding out about other people; the second is about remembering their names.

TASK 1 Getting to know each other
Sit together in a circle. Members of the group each choose someone not previously known to them and spend five minutes asking them about themselves. You could find out:

- why they are on the course;
- what they hope to get out of the course;
- what changes they have had to make to their lives in order to follow the course;
- about their interests and family life.

Now, reverse the process and answer the other person's questions about yourself. Go back into the full circle. Each member of the group, in turn, introduces the person whom they have been talking to, and tells the rest of the group something about this person.∎

TASK 2 Learning names
You will need a cushion or a soft ball for this activity.

Stand in a circle with the others in the group. Throw the cushion to someone in the group. As you throw it, call out your own name. Continue this until everyone has had a turn at calling out their own name at least twice.

Stay in the circle, and this time as you throw the cushion call out the name of the person to whom you are throwing it.

Now sit down in the circle and see whether you can remember everyone's name and something about each person.∎

Caring is about *people*. Each and every person is special in their own way. Whoever you are working with, or providing care for, you should be aware that these people have qualities and characteristics special to them as individuals.∎

1 • Knowing your GNVQ

This chapter considers the General National Vocational Qualification (GNVQ). In it, you will:

- gain an understanding of what is meant by health and social care, and be able to check that you have made an appropriate choice of study;
- be introduced to the GNVQ as a framework for vocational education and training;
- begin to take responsibility for your own learning.

Like the Introduction, this chapter is aimed at the reader who may not be absolutely sure what is involved in studying for a GNVQ in Health and Social Care. Those with previous knowledge and experience of GNVQs and/or working in health and social care should read and absorb what they need from this chapter, while also making sure that they are familiar with the contents of all of its sections.

WHAT IS HEALTH AND SOCIAL CARE?

Health and social care is concerned with people. Essentially it is about two groups of people: those who need care, and those who provide care.

However, this explanation is too simplistic and does not give the complete picture or tell the whole story. Which people, for example, need special care arrangements? What kind of care do they need? Who does the caring? What sort of care do the carers provide? Where does the caring take place?

The people who need care

Those in need of care are people who, for whatever reason, are unable to look after themselves independently. No doubt you can think of such people from your own life and experience. You may know older people who live in a residential home because they are no longer able to look after themselves. Or you may know older people who are able to remain in their own home, but only because they receive support. You may know, too, of younger people – single-parent families, for example – whose situations prevent them from leading independent lives. Spend a

People who need care and people who provide care

few minutes exchanging your experiences of such people with other members of your group.

Categories of need

People's care needs are varied and complex. Because of this, those in need of care have in the past been grouped into different categories according to their needs and circumstances. Six categories of need have been used:

- families with children;
- people with acute physical illness;
- people with physical disabilities;
- people with mental health difficulties;
- older people;
- people with special learning-support needs.

A drawback of using groupings such as these to define people's needs is that they encourage attempts to fit all of an individual's needs into one or other of the categories. In reality, a person's needs may fall into several categories, or into none of them. This highlights the importance of the point made at the end of the last chapter: caring is about *people*. It is not about categories of need, or trying to put people into the right boxes for classification. More will be said about this in Chapter 4: in the meantime, this presents a first opportunity to involve you in your own learning.

TASK *Identifying needs*

Think back to the people you identified a few moments ago as in need of care. Take each one of them in turn, and try to classify the person according to one or more of the six categories listed above.

Then think about each of the people again, this time as individuals. Try to picture for yourself what you consider their major needs to be. What are the main differences between the two approaches? Were there any individual needs that you could not classify? If so, what kind of needs were they, and why might they be difficult to classify? You may find it helpful to discuss your general findings with the rest of your group.■

This task should have helped you to understand what we mean when we say that everyone is special.

Carers and care workers

We have already used the terms *carer* and *care worker* without saying exactly what is meant by them. There is a difference.

It's unlikely that you managed to identify and discuss examples of people in need of care without at the same time talking about the people who respond to their care needs. All those involved in the *caring* of others are entitled to be called **carers**, whether they are family friends or professional members of the health and care services. A **care worker** is someone who provides care as a professional employee of the health and care services.

The difference between carers and care workers is often more about status and name than about the tasks that they perform. Often, the care the groups provide may be very similar; the real distinction is that the care worker is part of a professional team, and is trained and employed to provide care to those in need. As a result care workers will find themselves providing care in many different situations and circumstances, as well as in a variety of places or care settings. These could include caring for people in their own homes, in residential settings such as hospitals or nursing homes, or in day or activity centres, or family centres.

So far we have referred to carers and care workers as 'people' or 'workers'. In fact, they are the women and

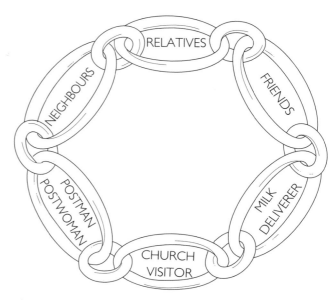

Some of the people who make up the chain of care providers

men carrying out the varied roles and duties related to caring. The larger proportion of workers in the caring services are women, but in principle this need not be so – all of the roles and responsibilities involved in caring can just as easily be carried out by men as by women. For this reason care workers and others will sometimes be referred to in the book as 'she' and sometimes as 'he'.

Teamwork

Care workers as a group do not work alone. They are one part of a larger team of professionals who together provide care for people in need. Others in the team may be more familiar to you: nurses, doctors and social workers, for example. Whoever they are, it is important that they work together as a group, each supporting the efforts and skills of the other.

All carers, whether paid professionals or not, have important roles to play. Those who provide care as friends, neighbours and family are just as important as everyone else. You will quickly discover what an important link they are in the chain of care providers.

CARING IN ACTION

Another way to get to grips with what is involved in health and social care is to take a look at it in action. Here are three brief episodes or **case studies** which focus attention on three separate people. These people happen to be in the same place at the same time, although in very different circumstances. Read each episode through a couple of times, so that you have a general picture of what has happened and the circumstances surrounding each of the central characters.

Episode 1

A serious road traffic accident has occurred in a busy street. A middle-aged man has been struck by a motor car and is lying in the road. The emergency services have arrived; they include paramedic staff, who give the man emergency treatment. He is taken by ambulance to the casualty department of the local hospital and later undergoes surgery before being transferred to a specialist ward.

Episode 2

In the same accident an elderly woman has suffered abrasions and cuts to her legs and forearms. She is not seriously injured, and is taken to the same hospital and treated for her physical injuries as an out-patient. She is then sent home. She lives alone but has a married daughter who lives two miles away.

Episode 3

As the accident was happening a young mother was coming out of her flat onto the street in question. With her are her three children, aged between 15 months and 5 years of age, the baby having been born with a congenital condition called Down's syndrome. They are on their way to the family day centre.

TASK Provision of care

Spend 15 minutes or so thinking about, and discussing within your group, the following questions:

- What care needs can you identify in relation to the man and woman injured in the accident that have not already been identified in the description?
- What role(s) might a care worker play in meeting the needs of:
  - the man in the accident?
  - the woman in the accident?
  - the young mother who was passing by?
- What might the care services provide in order to meet the needs of the young mother and her children?■

OBSERVATIONS

You may by now be feeling that you did not have enough information to respond to the questions – if so, that's one useful lesson to have learned! Care workers need all the information they can get if they are to make appropriate and professional judgements about people's needs. Obtaining this information means asking questions in order to make sense of the situations we have to respond to.

In the case of the injured man you were probably looking for the following:

- How long is he likely to be in hospital?
- Does he have a wife and family at home?

- If so, do they live locally?
- What support might they need while he's in hospital?
- What support services would be available in the hospital?

In the case of the elderly woman, the lack of information about her circumstances makes it equally difficult to identify her care needs:

- What were her needs *before* the accident?
- Is she already being visited by a care worker?
- What injuries has she sustained and how will these affect her ability to manage at home by herself?
- Does she have helpful neighbours?
- Does she have a supportive relationship with her daughter?
- Would she qualify for any financial support?

The situation of the young mother presents much the same problems. Again, we need to know a great deal more about her circumstances before we could say with any confidence what support and help she might need or be entitled to.■

POINTS TO REMEMBER

So, what have we learned about health and social care and the job of the care worker? Look through the list of points given below and make sure that you understand the significance of each of them.

Working in health and social care is about:

- meeting the needs of individuals because *everyone* is special;
- making sense of care situations, which means obtaining all the information that you can;
- asking the right questions, and reaching decisions on the basis of your theoretical knowledge and practical experience;
- recognising that each caring situation is different because the circumstances of the people involved are different;
- understanding that providing care involves a great many people, from specialists in hospitals to friends and neighbours;
- recognising that each team member has a role to play – clearly the paramedics' role was critical in the action we have just considered, but so in its own way was the role of the married daughter in the case of the elderly woman;
- thinking and acting as a professional, and doing one's best in the circumstances.

Working in health and social care is *not* about:

- trying to fit people into categories in order to make sense of, and to respond to, their needs;
- looking for ready-made answers to people's situations and needs.■

THE GNVQ: A PROFESSIONAL QUALIFICATION IN CARING

How can you become a qualified care worker? That's where the GNVQ comes in. Studying and training to be a professional employee in health and social care means obtaining a qualification. This you can do through a GNVQ.

The GNVQ awards were set up by the Government to create nationally recognised courses of study and training leading to qualifications in particular occupational areas, such as manufacturing, leisure and tourism, business, and your own area – health and social care. Because these qualifications are directly related to particular areas of employment, they are **vocational** – they involve education and training designed for particular jobs in a chosen vocation, or profession.

Levels of qualification

There are three levels of GNVQ available at present:

- Foundation;
- Intermediate;
- Advanced.

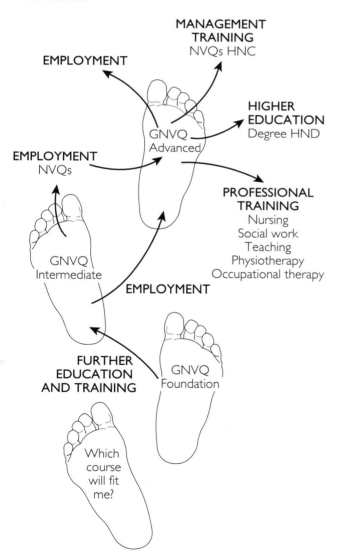

Opportunities offered by GNVQ courses

If you have already taken a Foundation level GNVQ as a step towards taking the Intermediate level GNVQ you will know that taking a GNVQ does not necessarily mean going straight into employment. As the diagram below shows, the GNVQ courses offer you choices.

Where do GNVQs lead?

GNVQs are designed to prepare you for:

- further study and training in health and social care;
- employment in health and social care;
- further study in higher education.

This means that you can use them as preparation for taking further GNVQ courses. Also, a qualification at Advanced level can be used in a similar way to apply for admission into higher education, where you can continue your studies. Lastly, a GNVQ award can be used to gain employment in health and social care.

Intermediate level

Look again at the steps diagram (opposite) and remind yourself where the GNVQ at Intermediate level fits into this progressive approach towards obtaining qualifications. You will see that the Intermediate level qualification forms the third step in the pathway and will provide you with two choices when successfully completed:

- you can go on to the next step and study for an Advanced GNVQ in Health and Social Care;
- you can look for employment in health and social care.

Chapter 2 gives detailed information about the GNVQ in Health and Social Care at Intermediate level.

STUDYING FOR THE GNVQ

Thinking for yourself

Because no two situations that you will meet will ever be exactly alike, it is vital that you learn to think for yourself as part of your training programme. Being told what to do in one situation is no guarantee that you will know what to do in another situation. Remember that each situation has its own individual and special circumstances.

This approach to learning was referred to earlier as **learning through doing**. It was also described as **independent learning** or **reflective learning**. All mean the same thing: making you an active participant in your own learning. On page 7 you were asked to reflect upon the exercise you had just done. This was only another way of saying 'think for yourself' about what you had just done.

As you go through your course you will find this approach being used a great deal. You will frequently be asked to carry out **tasks** and **activities** designed to help you develop and improve your practical knowledge, skills and experience. For example, you will be expected:

- to search for information that is relevant to the health and social care units;
- to make links between what you do in the workplace and your work at college or school;
- to show initiative by setting personal goals for your own learning.

Getting help and support

Tutors will give you help to achieve the expectations listed above. They will help you to link observations and practice in the workplace with the theory of health and social care introduced in the GNVQ course. You will also be given help on how to use journals, textbooks, case studies and assignments in order to learn about health and social care. Sometimes you will be expected to work alone; at other times you will be working with other students, or with people who supervise you when you are in the workplace.

Although you will have a **course tutor** who oversees your work and progress, there will also be a team of **specialist staff** teaching the GNVQ in Health and Social Care. They will use a variety of teaching methods to help you to learn what you need to know and to reflect on what you have learned.

Learning for yourself

Learning for yourself is not an easy option. You will most likely enjoy the freedom of making decisions that will affect you directly and cope well with the challenge. But taking responsibility for your own learning means being good at managing your own time. How good are you at this?

- Do you tend to put things off until the last minute?
- Do you sit talking with friends when you know you have a deadline to meet for an assignment?

If you are always running late, or frequently having to negotiate with your tutor about handing in an overdue assignment, then you should review your commitments. You may have to decide to put an outside activity to one side in order to meet the demands of your studies.

Managing your own time

Of course you should be enjoying yourself and taking part in all kinds of activities, but keep in mind the advantages of:

- recognising when you need to ask for help;
- knowing where to go to find help when you do need it;
- keeping to deadlines set by tutors.

You should also know where you can find **resources** which will help you with your work. Knowing how to make effective use of the **library** is a skill you will often need. At the beginning of your course you will be introduced to the many ways a library can help you with your work (see also Chapter 8).

Why choose the GNVQ in Health and Social Care?

The Intermediate GNVQ in Health and Social Care has three main attractions:

- It is a vocational qualification that is recognised nationally.
- It can lead directly to a job, such as care assistant or family helper, or to further study at GNVQ Advanced level.
- It can be studied on a part-time basis by those already in employment.

During the GNVQ you will have the chance to observe people working in the field of health and social care and this will help you to make up your mind about the area of caring in which you may want to specialise. Possibilities include work with:

- older people;
- children;
- families;
- people with physical disabilities;
- people with mental health difficulties;
- people with chronic illnesses;
- people with acute physical illnesses;
- people with special or additional learning needs.

Try to get as many different working experiences as possible, so that you can make an informed decision about what you want to do in the future. Your work for the Health and Social Care GNVQ will also help you to make your choice.

KEY WORDS AND TECHNICAL TERMS

Day centre or activity centre A place that people can visit during the day. Some centres provide leisure activities, others offer general care facilities.

Down's syndrome An abnormality in which a child is born with an extra chromosome (47 instead of 46). People with Down's syndrome have a characteristic physical appearance and varying degrees of learning difficulty.

Family centre A place that provides facilities for parents and their children to meet socially within the community. Such centres are often housed within local community centres (see page 37).

Health and care services A wide range of different services which exist to support the health and care needs of the population. They are made up of *people*, such as doctors, nurses, social workers and care workers; *facilities*, such as hospitals, surgeries and health centres; and *organisations and agencies*, often voluntary, such as Age Concern, Children in Need, and the National Society for the Prevention of Cruelty to Children. (See Chapter 7.)

Paramedic A member of the health services trained in advanced resuscitation and life-support measures,

and ready to answer emergency calls and to treat casualties at the scene of emergencies such as road accidents.

Residential homes Homes for older people who are unable to look after themselves in their own homes; for young people who require care and protection; and for others with severe learning difficulties. Residential homes are staffed by social workers and care workers and form part of the health and care services.

Vocational education A programme of study and training specifically designed as preparation for a particular job or career.

2 • The GNVQ in Health and Social Care

This chapter looks at the GNVQ in Health and Social Care. You will:

- learn how the GNVQ in Health and Social Care at Intermediate level is made up;
- see how the different sections of the GNVQ in Health and Social Care contribute to the overall purpose of the course;
- be introduced to what is required to gain the GNVQ in Health and Social Care at Intermediate level;
- meet some of the technical terms used in the assessment of the GNVQ, and the part that they play in the GNVQ programme;
- be given an example of how core skills units are linked into the other units, and how they are assessed.

THE GNVQ JIGSAW

The GNVQ in Health and Social Care at Intermediate level is made up of two areas of study:

- health and social care;
- core skills.

Both these areas are divided into **units** of study. A unit is the basic building block within the GNVQ programme. Each unit provides a separate block of study with its own requirements in terms of the knowledge, skills and values to be learned and assessed. Each unit has also been designed to link into the programme as a whole: this means that what you learn in one unit will help you in other units. Like a jigsaw puzzle, the separate pieces fit together to give a complete picture.

In the case of your Intermediate GNVQ programme there are nine pieces in the jigsaw – nine separate units that you must study and be assessed on. Six of these units are in the area of health and social care and three are in the area of core skills. As the diagram on page 13 shows, the units in the health and social care area are divided into two groups:

- 4 mandatory units;
- 2 optional units.

Health and social care units

The purpose of the **health and social care units** is to give you an understanding of the specialist or theoretical knowledge you need to become a care worker.

You need to be aware of two differences between the mandatory units and the optional units. The first is that you *must* study the **mandatory** units whereas you have a *choice* about which **optional** units you will study. The same four mandatory units are offered to all students taking the GNVQ in England and Wales: in other words, you have to do the same four mandatory units whichever school or college you attend. The second difference is that the four optional units are offered by three different awarding bodies: the Business and Technology Education Council (BTEC), City and Guilds, and the Royal Society of Arts (RSA). Your school or college will be registered with *one* of these awarding bodies and you will make your choice of optional units from those on offer in your school or college.

The units in health and social care are as follows:

- Mandatory units:
  - Unit 1: Promoting Health and Well-Being.
  - Unit 2: Influences on Health and Well-Being.
  - Unit 3: Health and Social Care Services.
  - Unit 4: Communication and Inter-personal Relationships in Health and Social Care.
- Optional units:
  - Choose two units from those offered by BTEC, City and Guilds, or RSA.

Core skills units

The purpose of the **core skills units** is to help you gain some of the practical skills needed by a professional and efficient care worker. These are skills that you will need in almost all aspects of your work, which is why they are called *core* skills. The core of something – an apple, for instance – is the central part of the fruit which contains the seeds for future growth and development. In much the same way you need to have a central core of skills in order to develop as a good care worker.

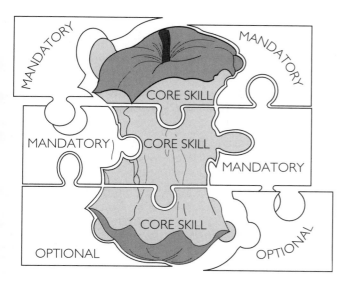

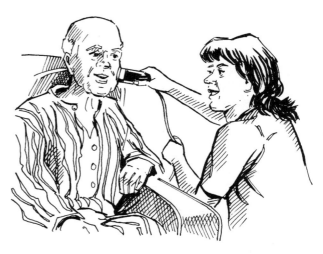

The nine pieces of the jigsaw that make up the GNVQ

Communicating through a smile

Because students studying for GNVQs in other vocational areas, such as business and engineering, require the same basic or core skills as you do, the core skills units are the same for all GNVQ courses. What makes them different for each of the GNVQ programmes of study is that they are closely linked to the units of that area of work: they are not studied separately. In your case they are linked to the health and social care units and you will be expected to show that you have acquired the necessary core skills through the assignment work in these units. An example of how this works in practice is given later in the chapter. Your tutors will also help you with this when you begin your studies of the health and social care units.

The core skills units are:

- Unit 1: Communication;
- Unit 2: Application of Number;
- Unit 3: Information Technology.

Using core skills

Communication is at the centre of our lives: it is what we spend a lot of our time doing. In caring it has a particularly important role to play, as the ability to do the job depends very much on the ability to talk and listen to people and to create relationships of confidence and trust. These rely on good communication skills. You will quickly come to realise, though, that communication doesn't mean *just* talking and listening to people – a smile, for example, is a simple form of communication, yet a very effective one. The point to remember is that communication is often taking place without us even knowing it.

The ability to communicate will also depend on other skills. Often we are not face to face with the person or persons with whom we wish to communicate. For

example, we may be communicating by telephone, in which case we can't any longer rely on a smile to communicate confidence and trust. Alternatively, it may mean communicating through the written word in the form of a letter, a report or a brief note. This might mean using a computer, which could in turn mean collecting and storing information for later use. Many of you may already be familiar with computers, or what we more generally call **information technology**; if so, you will know that using this form of communication requires special skills and abilities.

Finally, words, whether spoken or written, are not the only means we use to organise our lives and affairs. To give and receive some information, to decide whether we can afford something, to grade an assignment, and so on, we use **numbers**. The messages and information communicated through numbers are also an important part of our daily lives and an important part of a job in health and social care. For example, suppose you had to decide how much care someone might need. Would your decision be based solely on health and care grounds, or would it also be a matter of financial calculation – what it would cost, and how much money was available?

What's in the core skills units?

Care workers need to have or develop a variety of personal skills. In general, skills are the things that we can *do*, and are able to *show* that we can do. Recall the difference between theoretical knowledge and practical knowledge: practical knowledge is about knowing how to do something in practice, which means both *possessing* and *using* the appropriate personal skills to get the job done. This is the thinking behind the core skills units, which pick out very precisely the skills needed to do the job. The following list gives you an idea of the kinds of skills involved in each of the three units.

- Unit 1: Communication
  - take part in discussions on straightforward subjects in different situations and with different people;
  - produce written material on straightforward subjects which is appropriate for the audience and its purpose;
  - use images such as diagrams, photographs and pictures to illustrate points in both written materials and discussions;
  - read and respond to written materials in order to obtain and extract relevant information.

- Unit 2: Application of Number
  - collect and record data through a range of simple data-collection and measuring tasks;
  - tackle problems using a series of techniques which employ calculator and non-calculator methods;
  - interpret and present data identifying the main features and showing how these relate to the problem tackled.

- Unit 3: Information Technology
  - prepare information appropriate to a task and enter it using the software and make decisions about the most appropriate way to store the input and make backup copies;
  - process information required for a task and edit and reorganise it as appropriate;
  - present information appropriate to a range of different situations and purposes;
  - evaluate the use of information technology compared with other methods of working which might have been used.

You may already have many of these skills. If so – good! The point of the core skills units is to pick out the skills you are expected to have, and to give you the chance to show that you have them through your work and learning on the course. You yourself take responsibility for showing that you can meet the requirements of the core skills units (see Chapter 3).

★ ★ ★ REVIEW POINT ★ ★ ★

Take a moment to check through what you have learned so far in this chapter. **Reviewing** your own learning in this way can be achieved by giving yourself a short test. Before going on to the next section try answering the following questions without looking back to the relevant pages.

- What are the health and social care units?
- What are the core skills units?
- What is the difference between the mandatory and the optional units in the health and social care area of study?
- How many optional units will you study?

Now look back and check that you've got the answers right!

GETTING THE QUALIFICATION

This section looks at what you have to do to gain a GNVQ at Intermediate level in Health and Social Care. It introduces you to some terms which may be new to you if you are studying a GNVQ for the first time. Read it through fairly quickly first time round, but before going on to Chapter 3 come back and read it again so that you are well prepared for the information in Chapter 3. If you have studied for a GNVQ before, you may wish to go straight to Chapter 4.

Grades of qualification

There are three **grades** of qualification which you can be awarded on successful completion of the GNVQ. These awards are:

- pass;
- pass with merit;
- pass with distinction.

Each of these grades requires that you achieve a particular level of performance: these levels are called **standards**. To gain a pass award you have to reach a particular standard of work which will be the same for all students taking the GNVQ and will be known and understood by employers. The standard required to get a merit award is more demanding than that required to get a pass, and a distinction award is even more challenging. Chapter 3 tells you more about what's involved in each of the grades.

Crediting completed units

If for some reason you do not complete all the units in the course, you will still be entitled to receive a **certificate** crediting you with the units that you have successfully completed. This is important to know, as this certificate can be used to show that you have passed these units should you decide to start the course again at a later date.

The pass award

The requirements for achieving a pass award will give you some idea of what is involved in completing the course successfully. (How you achieve these requirements is described in Chapter 3.) In order to gain a pass you are required to:

- Cover all the work and complete the assignments at pass standard in:
  - 3 core skills units;
  - 4 mandatory units;
  - 2 optional units.
- Pass tests in:
  - mandatory unit 1;
  - mandatory unit 2;
  - mandatory unit 3.

Tests

Tests are used in three of the mandatory units (Units 1, 2 and 3) to see whether you have reached the required standard of achievement in these units. The purpose of the tests is not to find out which of you is best in your group: their sole purpose is to allow you to show that you personally have reached the necessary standard, or, alternatively, to discover that there are still some things you need to do.

These tests are not set by your tutors: they are set externally by City and Guilds, BTEC or RSA. Your college or school will have chosen the awarding body which will provide the tests.

ASSESSMENT

Tests provide only one way of finding out whether you have achieved the required standard. Another is through the work you do and record as you proceed through the course. This **assessed work**, when it has all been put together, counts as your overall **assessment** for the course.

Each unit you study has to be completed and assessed as part of the total assessment for the GNVQ before you can be awarded your qualification. It is this assessed work, along with the tests, which provides most of the **evidence** used to judge whether you have reached the required standard of achievement.

Assessed work

Assessed work is the work you do as part of your ongoing studies and training. The following list provides *examples* of assessed work:

- assignments;
- displays;
- reports;
- practical demonstrations and presentations;
- projects;
- notes on observations;
- logbooks/diaries;
- case studies.

Further information about many of these can be found in Chapter 3. You will quickly become familiar with them once you get started.

Evidence

In order to know whether you have reached a given standard or not, **evidence** or proof of this is needed. Remember, it is the assessed work that provides most of this evidence, so the grade of qualification you achieve is very much in your own hands. The evidence is used for two purposes. Firstly, it will show whether you have completed *all* the work required, and secondly, it will provide the basis for making a judgement about the quality of your performance in terms of the three grades of award: pass, merit and distinction. More is said about this in Chapter 3.

The portfolio

The responsibility for collecting, recording and presenting the evidence that will be used to assess your performance is yours. This brings us to another word you need to be familiar with early on in your studies – **portfolio**. The portfolio is a file or collection of information which you can carry with you. This is also a good description of the part it plays in your studies. The portfolio is a file or folder containing the evidence you will collect and take with you throughout the course of your studies. It will include the assessed work in each of the Mandatory, Optional and Core Skills units, and any other materials that you feel may help provide evidence upon which to judge the standard of your performance. The illustration on page 16 gives you an idea of the kinds of things which you are likely to collect as evidence to include in your portfolio.

Because putting together the portfolio is *your* responsibility, it plays an important part in developing your ability to take an active role in your own learning. You have to decide what counts as evidence, which means that you have to make judgements about your own performance. This is known as **self-assessment** – that is, looking at yourself in terms of how you are getting on: what you do well; what you do less well; what you need to do to improve your performance; and how you go about it. You are in the best position to answer these questions.

The portfolio is, therefore, a personal record of the work you have carried out while studying for your GNVQ. It is a working file that you can add to throughout your studies and which can be a useful reference for employers or when applying for further courses of study. You will receive further help and guidance with the portfolio as you read through this book and as you get started with the course.

★ ★ ★ REVIEW POINT ★ ★ ★

Try to answer the following questions. Go back to the book when you need to.

1 How many grades of GNVQ qualification are there? What are they?

2 What is a GNVQ certificate and why might it be useful to you?

3 What do you have to do to gain a GNVQ pass award?

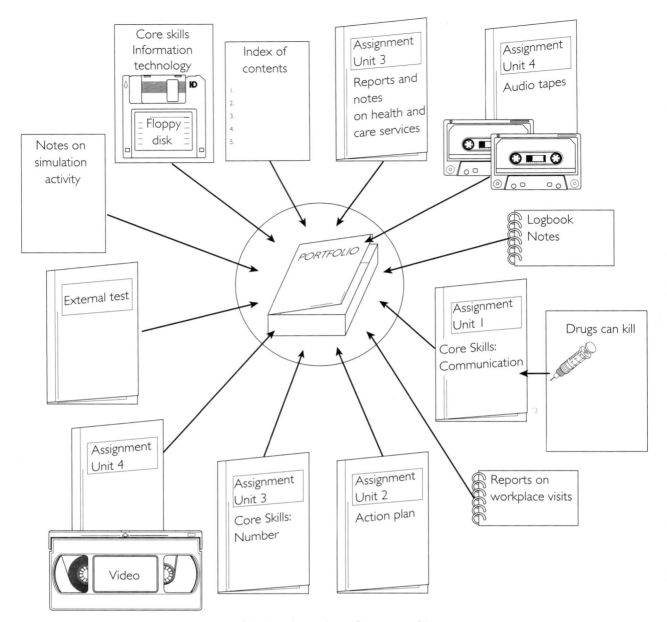

Collecting the evidence for your portfolio

4 What is a test?

5 What is meant by evidence in a GNVQ?

6 What is a portfolio? How is it used?

STANDARDS

Standards define what is required to pass the course and gain a GNVQ award, or to do even better and gain a merit or distinction award. We have already stressed the key role played by evidence in judging whether you have reached the required standard, and we have referred to your own role in providing that evidence through your portfolio. But how do you, the person being assessed, know what is meant by work or performance of the right standard? All we've said so far is that there is a common standard, fixed nationally.

For many of the tasks we undertake, defining the standard required of us is a relatively easy matter. For

instance, if there is only one possible answer or outcome to a task that we are asked to perform, either we complete it successfully or we fail to complete it. In other words we either get the answer right or else we get it wrong. In this type of task the standard is defined as achieving the right answer.

But as we've seen, *caring* is not like this; nor are most jobs that involve working with people. As a care worker there will be a variety of answers to most of the problems and situations you'll be expected to tackle. This means that the answers are often only as good as the thinking that lies behind them. *How* you arrive at an answer is often as important as the answer itself.

To illustrate this, think about how you might decide on the best route when driving to a holiday destination. In all likelihood there will be more than one possible route, and some may clearly be better than others. The thinking behind your planning will

Time to think again!

be important. For instance, is the shortest route necessarily the quickest route? What would be the best time of day to travel? Do you know of any roadworks on the routes which you might otherwise choose?

The thinking behind the decisions you make once your journey is underway will be just as important. As we know, not everything always goes according to plan. How would you cope with circumstances which you could not have anticipated, e.g. a breakdown, a traffic jam, a diversion, and so on? Finally, the decisions you make in relation to the return journey in the light of your experiences of the outward journey will also be significant. In each case the outcome is likely to be only as good as the thinking which lies behind your actions.

The same holds true for the care worker. The thinking behind your actions will often be developed over a period of time as the circumstances change around you. When this happens your first plan of action may well not match what you finally do. You will need to be flexible and prepared to adapt in order to take into account factors you could not have anticipated at the outset.

How do we define a good journey?

Suppose when you arrived at your holiday destination you were asked whether you'd had a good trip. What factors would you need to consider in coming to an answer? Would you be able to say that you'd had a good trip simply because you had reached your destination? Or would you also want to take into account the actual experience of the journey itself? Both factors would be relevant: neither on its own would be sufficient. To have had a good journey yet to have arrived at the wrong destination would not count as a good trip, nor would arriving very late at the right destination because you had got lost several times on the way.

This indicates what is involved in defining the standards expected of you in the GNVQ. Because there are many possible outcomes or answers to the situations you will face as a care worker, the same two

factors come into play when defining the standards expected of you. You will need to provide two sorts of evidence. First, you will need to show that you have reached the destination, or outcomes required of you – that you have acquired certain knowledge, skills and attitudes. Second, you will need to show that you are able to use these in different situations, providing evidence of your thinking, your decision making, your communication skills, and so on.

It is difficult to define the precise standards expected of you in the second of these assessment areas. Consider the holiday example again.

TASK *Assessing a journey*
Think back to the travelling part of the journey. What information or evidence would you need in order to say whether the journey had been a good one? If you can, think about this as a group activity.

Make a list of the kinds of questions you would ask about the journey in deciding on the quality of the journey. Then compare your list with the one provided at the end of this chapter.▮

OBSERVATIONS
Though your list will no doubt include questions that differ from the ones provided, they should be along the same lines. They should all be attempting to get *behind* the activity or task itself and to look at the thinking, the decision making, the planning and the learning from experience that went into achieving the intended outcome. We have described a professional as a person able to apply her or his theoretical knowledge, practical skills and experience to respond to complex situations. It is *your* use of these abilities that in the end defines the quality of your performance.

In the GNVQ programme, just completing the assignments and tasks won't by itself be enough to demonstrate that you have achieved the required standard. It will be important also that you provide evidence to show how you arrived at your conclusions – how you used your knowledge, skills and experience to respond to the assignments you were asked to carry out.▮

ACHIEVING THE STANDARDS

The remainder of this chapter, together with Chapter 3, explain how to achieve the required standard for a GNVQ. The sections in this chapter concentrate on what is expected of you in terms of the knowledge, skills and values to be learned or developed, and on how you will be helped to acquire these through the way in which the units are arranged and made up. Chapter 3 then looks at how these abilities are assessed.

Technical terms are used in these sections which may be new to you. You will soon become familiar with these terms and the process of GNVQ assessment.

Units and elements

First, let's look at the way the GNVQ programme identifies the standards expected of you. Think back a moment to what was said earlier about the overall assessment of the GNVQ. You are required to achieve a certain standard in each of the nine units you study. All the assessed work – in the form of the evidence you will present in your portfolio – will count towards your assessment in each of the units in health and social care and in the core skills. For each of these you therefore need a clear definition of the standard to be reached in each assignment or other assessment task.

Let's see how this works in practice. The starting-point is the unit. The description we used earlier is this:

> ‘A unit is the basic building block within the GNVQ programme. Each unit provides a separate block of study, with its own requirements in terms of the knowledge, skills and values to be learned and assessed.’

The content of each unit is described by the unit title. For example, Unit 1 has the title ‘Promoting Health and Well-Being’, and covers the whole area of life-saving skills and the promotion of health behaviours. To reach a satisfactory standard in this area you need a wide variety of knowledge and practical skills. Unit 4 is ‘Communication and Inter-personal Relationships in Health and Social Care’: this covers what you need to be aware of, and do, to give someone emotional support. This is a somewhat different type of unit, and demands a high level of personal understanding and sensitivity in terms of communications skills and personal values.

Defining the standards within each of these units is made easier for you by breaking them down into **elements**, each element defining a separate block of knowledge, skills and values to be learned and assessed. Elements are like miniature building blocks, smaller than units but similar in the way they are organised and constructed.

For example, Unit 4, ‘Communication and Inter-personal Relationships in Health and Social Care’, is made up of three elements, each with a title of its own:

Unit 4: Communication and Inter-personal Relationships in Health and Social Care

- Element 4.1: Develop communication skills;
- Element 4.2: Explore how inter-personal relationships may be affected by discriminatory behaviour;
- Element 4.3: Investigate aspects of working with clients in health and social care.

Each element in the unit must be passed in order to pass the unit as a whole. Remember, it's your responsibility to provide the evidence showing that you have reached the required standard in each element, but this means that you in turn need a clear indication of what this standard involves. GNVQ uses some technical terms to help you to understand this process.

Performance criteria

Let's use Element 4.1 in Unit 4 as an example.

The title of Element 4.1 is ‘Develop communication skills’. This tells you what you must *do* in the element, but not what particular knowledge or skills are involved in doing this. The title tells you the destination you must reach, but doesn't tell you the particular knowledge, skills and values you must demonstrate in reaching that destination. These are defined by what are called **performance criteria**.

Each element has a series of performance criteria which explain in more detail what is involved in meeting the requirements of that element. Thus, for Element 4.1 the performance criteria say that you must:

- explain why it is important for individuals, families and groups to *communicate*;
- demonstrate *listening* and *responding* skills to encourage communication with individuals in different contexts;
- demonstrate *observation* skills to encourage communication with individuals in different contexts;
- identify *obstacles* to effective communication;
- *evaluate* one's own communication skills and make suggestions for their improvement.

Each of these criteria covers a broad area of skill or knowledge. There are, for example, many conversational techniques, some more appropriate in some circumstances than others: which you need when is for you to decide. To help you, statements (or clues) are given. These identify for you the particular areas in which you might look for information, skill or evidence that is most relevant. These statements together indicate the **range**.

Range

To understand the term ‘range’ think about and compare things that are within your range and things that are outside your range. Those within your range are the things that you can see, hear, smell or touch because you are close enough to do so. Similarly, you are able to buy something you want if the price is within the range you can afford. Things that are in range are the ones you can respond to because you have the necessary information, money, visual image, and so on to help you. Things out of your range cannot be responded to in the same way – for example, it is difficult to respond to something you cannot see clearly, or to buy something outside your price range.

In GNVQ, the range statements tell you what is 'in range' in terms of the performance criteria – that is, they tell you from which areas you should draw your evidence. For Element 4.1, the areas identified as being within range in terms of responding to the performance criteria listed above are these:

- *Important for*: development of self, personal beliefs and preferences, development of groups/ families.
- *Listening and responding skills*: facial expression, body language, eye contact, sensory contact, posture, minimal prompts, paraphrasing, summarising, questioning, tone, pitch, pace of communication.
- *Contexts*: one-to-one, groups of three or more, peer group, groups which include individuals of different status.
- *Observational skills*: verbal behaviour, non-verbal behaviour, appearance.
- *Obstacles*: environmental, social and cultural constraints.
- *Evaluate* in terms of: self-assessment, feedback from others, suggesting improvements in others.

This still leaves you with the task of weighing up the relative importance of the evidence you come across in each of these areas. You haven't been given the answer, rather guided towards the things you need to think about. Further help in deciding what evidence will be most useful is given in the form of **evidence indicators**.

Evidence indicators

Evidence indicators give you an idea of what types of evidence you should be looking for in the range of areas identified. In the case of Element 4.1, 'Develop communication skills', the evidence indicators are:

'Records of interactions carried out in two settings, one of which is one-to-one and the other involving a group. One context should also involve at least one person who is of a different status to the student. Each assessment should include an evaluation by someone other than the student, and a self-assessment by the student as to the quality of their communication and how s/he could make improvements in the future.'

The language used in this description is taken from a GNVQ publication and will be explained to you more fully by your teachers and tutors. You will soon get used to the language once you start to use it in practice.

PUTTING THE JIGSAW TOGETHER AGAIN

In this chapter we have taken apart the GNVQ in Health and Social Care, and looked at each piece separately to see how it works and how it fits into the overall picture of the GNVQ. In the first section of the chapter we compared this with a jigsaw puzzle: each individual piece in the puzzle, as well as having its own place in the picture, links neatly with the others – each piece helps to build up the complete picture. The number of pieces in the puzzle has now increased significantly, with each piece having been carefully described so that a new and rather more detailed picture has emerged. Here we have used words to communicate this information. Earlier (in the diagram on p.13) we showed how such information could be communicated in a visual form.

CORE SKILLS IN ACTION

Different forms of communication were identified earlier in the chapter. One of these, in the core skills unit 'Communication', was about using images such as pictures and diagrams to highlight the written word. This was taken from Element 2.3, 'Use Images', which expects you to be able to:

'use images to illustrate points on straightforward matters in both written materials and discussions. The images used are appropriate to the audience, whether this is people familiar with the subject who know the student or people familiar with the subject who do not know the student.'

This chapter of the book has made use of images such as diagrams and pictures to illustrate the text and to help you understand what is being said. This is an example of how the core skills units work in the GNVQ. Remember, the core skills are learned and assessed *through* the health and social care units, not separately from them.

Imagine that this chapter represents an assignment carried out as part of one of the health and social care units. You would now be in a position to identify a selection of these pictures and diagrams as evidence of your ability to use the core skill outlined in Element 2.3 of the core skills unit, 'Communication'. This evidence you would present for assessment as part of the assignment, not separately from it, together with an explanation of how in your view it meets the requirements of Element 2.3.

This would all then become part of the collection of evidence kept and recorded in your **portfolio**, to be presented for assessment at the end of the GNVQ programme. However, because the evidence for the core skills will not be neatly collected together in one place in your portfolio, you will also need to provide an **index** showing where in the portfolio the evidence for the core skills units can be found. This personal responsibility for identifying your own progress and performance, recording details of it, and making decisions about quality, together make up what we called self-assessment.

★ ★ ★ REVIEW POINT ★ ★ ★

It's tempting to give you another test at this point but maybe that wouldn't be fair since you were told at the beginning of the chapter that you should treat it as an introduction and as a source of reference.

Even so, you need to have a good grasp of how the GNVQ works before you go on to the next chapter. This means being absolutely clear about the material covered in the sections above.

To make sure that you *are* clear, complete the three tasks below. Refer back to the relevant sections of this chapter if you need to, and ask for help from your tutors where necessary. Remember that you are reviewing your knowledge and skills, not being tested. (Chapter 3 begins with a brief summary of what you've learned.)∎

TASK 1 Reviewing key terms
Below is a list of the key terms used in this chapter. None of them is explained here, as the meaning of each term has been given in this chapter. Write a sentence or two about each term, making clear its meaning in relation to your GNVQ programme.

Key words and technical terms:

- Assessed work
- Elements
- Evidence
- Evidence indicators
- GNVQ tests
- Performance criteria
- Portfolio
- Range statements
- Self-assessment
- Unit∎

TASK 2 Illustrating the GNVQ structure
In the section above, on 'Core skills in action', we drew your attention to the importance of being able to communicate information visually. Construct an illustration or diagram showing how the GNVQ is made up and how it works, using the information provided in this chapter. Include units, elements, performance criteria, range statements and evidence indicators.∎

TASK 3 Understanding elements
Think back to the holiday example used earlier and imagine that in one of the units there is an element with the title, 'Identify factors which influence making a journey'. List the kinds of performance criteria, range statements and evidence indicators you would expect to find within this element.∎

AFTERWORD

A word of encouragement, if you've found this chapter heavy going. Like all learning it is much easier to understand something when you're doing it than when you're talking or reading about it. Once you get started, things will become clear – they will, you could say, come into range.

Response to Task: Assessing a journey (pages 16 and 17)
1 How was the route decided upon?
2 Did the original plans work out? If not, why? What was the thinking behind the revised plans?
3 What information was needed to plan the journey?
4 How was the information obtained? Was this done easily?
5 How long did the journey take? How long was the journey planned to take?
6 What did the journey cost? Was the cost kept within the planned budget?
7 What was learned in terms of the return journey?
8 Did those making the journey find it an enjoyable experience? Would they do it again?∎

3 • Making the grade

This chapter builds on what you learned in Chapter 2. In particular it looks at how the knowledge, skills and understanding you have acquired are assessed. In this chapter, you will:

* build on the information about the GNVQ given in Chapter 2;
* be introduced to the requirements needed to achieve the grades of pass, merit and distinction in the GNVQ;
* be introduced to grading criteria and action plans, and shown how they work in the GNVQ;
* be made aware of the different types of assessment used to develop the skills and abilities required of a professional carer;
* be given some practical advice about how to present your work;
* be made aware of some of the people involved in the assessment of the GNVQ and what they do.

This chapter begins by asking you to review what you've learned so far.

★★★ REVIEW POINT ★★★

Look through the following list of points, and, with the help of the sentences that you wrote at the end of Chapter 2 about the technical terms used in that chapter, check that you understand what each of the points means. If you feel unsure about any of them, go back to Chapter 2. If necessary ask your tutor for help, or get help from a member of your group who has already taken a GNVQ.

* The outcome you are expected to reach in each element of a unit is described in the title. This tells you what you must achieve in order to complete the element.
* You are provided with help to achieve the outcome or outcomes required through performance criteria, which tell you what general areas of knowledge and skills are involved; through range statements, which give you more precise information about each of these areas; and through evidence indicators, which tell you what kinds of evidence you should be looking for.
* Achieving the outcome of a task is only part of what you will be assessed on. Because several outcomes or

answers are often possible, the way that you go about reaching your solution or outcome plays an important part in your assessment.
* Showing how you reached your outcome or answer requires evidence of how you tackled the problem, and what you learned from doing it.

THE JOB OF A CARE WORKER

This chapter concentrates on the last two points in the above list. It looks at how those who assess your work decide on the quality of your thinking, your decision making, your communication skills, and your professional attitudes. One way to approach this is to think about it from the employer's point of view. This also provides a further opportunity to get you involved in your own learning.

⟫ **TASK** *The role of the care worker*
Imagine that you are an employer with a vacancy for a newly qualified care worker. You have advertised the post and need to write a job description as part of the information to be sent out to the applicants.

Make a list of the abilities that you think the successful applicant ought to have in order to do the job. Try to think of at least seven abilities that seem to you to be crucial.

When you've done this, share your thoughts with others in the group and decide on an agreed list. Then compare your list with the one provided in the 'Observations' section at the end of this chapter. The two lists should be very similar: if they aren't, follow the instructions provided there.∎

Assessing the abilities needed

The activities and assignments you will be asked to carry out in the GNVQ are designed to help you develop these **abilities**. These are not tests to find out what you can't do: they are carefully prepared activities to present you with opportunities to show what you have learned and what you can do. This will be stressed by your tutors, and helps to explain why you are given such careful guidance and information about how these activities should be tackled.

Earlier we looked at the information and guidance provided in the GNVQ to help you to achieve the standards required in each unit. We compared these to steps which will guide you towards your outcome. A similar kind of arrangement is provided to make clear how the seven abilities identified in the job description for a care worker (listed on page 31), are assessed through the work that you do. If you look at these abilities closely you will find that it's possible to group them into four broad areas, or categories.

Areas	Abilities
Planning	1, 4, 5
Obtaining and using information	2, 3
Reflection or review	7
Quality of outcomes	6

By now each of the terms used above should be familiar to you. They reflect the same processes that we identified when looking at how we might assess the quality of a journey (Chapter 2). In organising the trip you must go through several stages of preparation before setting out for your destination. At some stage you must gather the information you need in order to plan your route. Having planned it you will make the actual journey, and having arrived at your destination you will review the journey.

It sounds straightforward, in theory. In practice it's unlikely to have been quite so straightforward. As we saw when we identified the six categories of need in Chapter 1, things seldom fall neatly into categories. The same is true in the case of the holiday example. Thus the planning and information-gathering stages may well have overlapped. Although it's true that you cannot start planning something until you have the information you need, it's also true that you may start planning something only to find that you need more information. Or you may not discover that you need further information until you are well into your journey, because at that stage something happens that you could not have anticipated and planned for.

The lesson to be learned is that in practice, or in action, the individual stages are unlikely to be separate from each other. You don't go through one stage at a time, completing one before you go on to the next. Although each stage requires you to have particular skills, knowledge or understanding, you will use these as and when they are needed, according to the type of task you are set or the situation you find yourself in.

The need to see activities and tasks as a whole, in an integrated way, is well illustrated by the part that reflection and review play in this process. You need to reflect on your progress *throughout* an activity; not just when you've finished. Remember: not everything goes according to plan. You need to be ready to alter your original plan if things don't turn out as you expected. This continual process of reflecting and adapting is called **monitoring**: it allows you to review your plan in the light of changed circumstances or new information. Monitoring progress and performance is something you need to be doing right up to the moment you finish a task or an activity.

Once the task is completed, however, it is important to step back from it – to review the whole experience, and to assess what you've learned from it. This is **evaluation**. It differs from monitoring in that it is carried out at the end of an activity. By this stage it is too late to change your plans for this activity, but you can learn from this experience and be better prepared next time you are faced with a similar situation.

Finally there is the finished article or *outcome*: what you produce as the result of all your efforts, your knowledge and your skills. It may take the form of a report, a care plan, a demonstration, or a presentation, for example; it may be produced in written form, or be spoken or presented visually. Whatever form it takes, it provides key evidence of your presentation and communication skills as well as of your knowledge and understanding of what the task involved. Always remember that first impressions have a powerful and lasting effect on people. Remember, too, that what you hand in for assessment reflects your thoughts and decisions at the end of this piece of learning, and reveals what you have learnt from the assignment or activity.

☞ POINTS TO REMEMBER

Each task or activity you are asked to undertake, and each problem you are asked to solve, will involve the use of particular skills, knowledge and abilities if you are to complete it satisfactorily.

Each task can be broken down into four stages that you must go through in order to produce an outcome or a solution. However, these stages are not separate from each other:

• Planning.
• Using information.
• Outcome.
• Review: monitoring and evaluation.

As we saw with the journey, these four stages can be broken down into two essential parts: the *doing* of the task or activity, and the *results* of what you have done. The doing of the task involves you in a continuous **process** of planning, finding and using information,

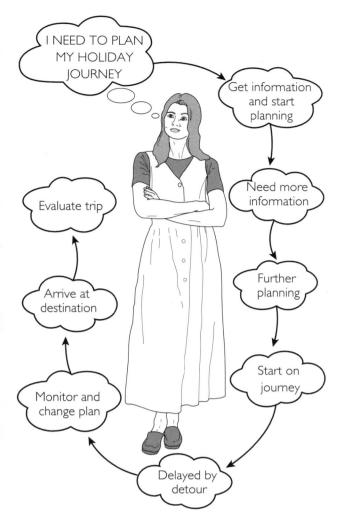

I NEED TO PLAN MY HOLIDAY JOURNEY

Get information and start planning

Need more information

Further planning

Start on journey

Delayed by detour

Monitor and change plan

Arrive at destination

Evaluate trip

The processes involved in tackling and solving a problem in practice

of reviewing your work so far, and of deciding what you still need to do (see the illustration above). The results of your efforts are the **outcome**.

Because more than one outcome is possible with so many of the tasks you will undertake, the way that you use your skills, knowledge and understanding to reach and to justify a particular outcome is important in assessing the quality of your performance. So, too, is the quality of the outcome itself. This distinction between the **processes** involved in solving a problem, and the **outcome** that results from them, provides a helpful basis for understanding how the GNVQ is assessed.

THEMES AND GRADING CRITERIA

In the GNVQ, assignments and tasks are broken down in order to assess the particular abilities that you must demonstrate. The same four stages are used for this purpose as those outlined above. The only difference is that the stages are called **themes**. These, too, divide into three **process** themes and an **outcome** theme. Their titles are:

Process

- Theme 1: Planning.
- Theme 2: Information seeking/handling.
- Theme 3: Evaluation.

Outcome

- Theme 4: Quality of outcomes.

Together these four themes provide a framework for assessing all of your work: each time you are given an activity or assignment to carry out it will be assessed in terms of the processes you go through in order to complete the task and the outcome(s) you produce. However, some themes may play a greater part in certain activities than in others, depending on the type of activity involved and the kind of learning it is designed to develop.

As you can see, each theme covers a very broad range of abilities. Because of this, you are provided with more precise information about what is expected within each theme. This information is offered as **grading criteria**. There are seven of these, divided between the four themes as follows:

Process

- *Theme 1: Planning*
  1 Drawing up plans of action.
  2 Monitoring courses of action.
- *Theme 2: Information seeking/handling*
  3 Identifying information needs.
  4 Identifying and using sources to obtain information.
- *Theme 3: Evaluation*
  5 Evaluating outcomes and justifying approaches.

Outcome

- *Theme 4: Quality of outcomes*
  6 How the piece of work as a whole fits together.
  7 Use of appropriate communication skills.

The word **grading** is simply another term for your work being assessed or marked. Each piece of work that you hand in will be assessed; at the end of the course, when you have completed all the assessed work, you will be given a final overall grade for the whole of the GNVQ.

The grading criteria help to identify what you must do to be awarded the GNVQ, and thus meet the requirements of the job description (page 21). They reflect the need for care workers to be people who can think for themselves and take an active part in their own learning and training. The criteria concentrate on:

Process

- how you go about your work;
- how much responsibility you take for your work;

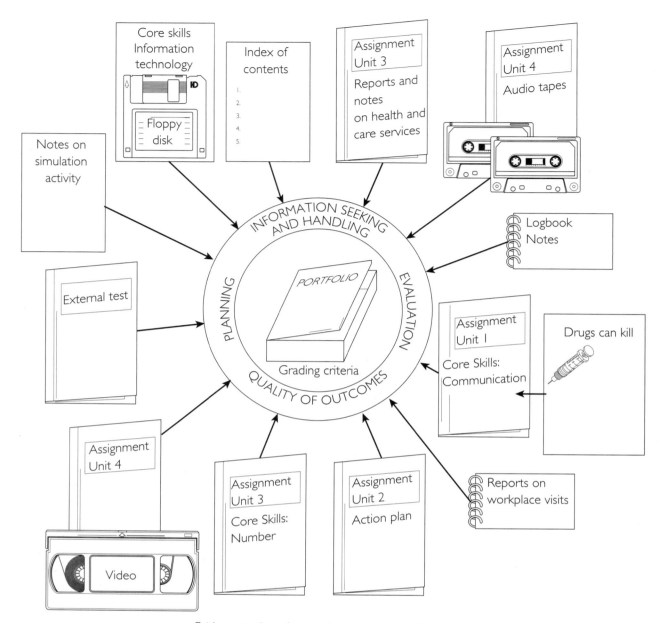

Evidence to show that you have met the grading criteria

- how you decide what information you need;
- how you find that information;
- how you monitor the progress of your plans;
- how you evaluate and review your performance;

organising an assignment in order to gather the evidence that you need.

Outcome

- the quality of the work that you actually produce (the quality of the outcomes).

The grading criteria identify abilities that you must show that you possess, so you need *evidence*. It is this evidence that is the basis for your final grade, so your portfolio is crucial. You need to gather evidence to show that you have met the grading criteria, as well as evidence relating to the mandatory, optional and core skills units. The diagram above reminds you how all of this fits together.

Now let's quickly review where we've got to, and then undertake a short task to check your understanding. After that, we shall look at how you go about

★ ★ ★ REVIEW POINT ★ ★ ★

Try to answer the following questions. Refer back to earlier sections of the chapter if you need to, or get help from your tutors or fellow students.

1 List the four themes in the GNVQ that cover the abilities you need to possess as a care worker.

2 List the grading criteria for each theme.

3 Identify the two kinds of review that are used.

4 Why is monitoring identified as a grading criterion under the theme of 'planning' rather than under the theme of 'evaluation'?

5 Why is the *quality* of what you produce important in the GNVQ?

TASK *Applying grading criteria*

This task is designed to show that you can apply your new knowledge. Once again, we use the holiday example.

Turn back to the list of questions we asked about the holiday on page 20. These questions were asked in order to obtain enough information to make a decision about the quality of the trip as a whole. Your task now is:

- to place each of the questions into one or other of the four GNVQ themes, and then identify which of the grading criteria within that theme has particular relevance;
- to present your findings clearly in a form that requires no spoken explanation – in other words, in a form that is self-explanatory to the reader.

When you have finished the task, turn to the 'Observations' section at the end of the chapter, and compare your own response with the one provided there. Read the comments about this task carefully before you go any further. Ask for help if you find there is anything that you don't understand.∎

ACTION PLANS

We now return to the question of how you go about organising an assignment or task in order to gather the evidence you need – evidence to demonstrate that you possess the necessary skills, knowledge and professional attitudes. This is called **action planning**.

For each assignment and activity you are asked to carry out, you will receive clear guidance about what is expected of you, and you will be given information about the relevant grading criteria. From this guidance and information you will be expected to produce an **action plan**, which shows how you intend to tackle the assignment. You will then discuss this with your tutor, and modify it if necessary.

An action plans serves three main purposes. First, it encourages you to think through what you are doing and what you plan to do, so that each part of an activity is carefully recorded and then reviewed. Secondly, the action plan provides evidence of how you tackled the assignment: this will be needed by the assessors in judging whether or not you have met the grading criteria. Thirdly, the process of devising an action plan is similar to the procedure you will be expected to follow as a care worker when preparing a care plan for a person in need. So, producing action plans helps to develop this professional skill.

Devising an action plan

Action plans can be designed in a number of ways. Your college or school may have a set design for you

to follow: in this case you will be told about this once you have been set an assignment, and given guidance by your teachers or tutors on how it works.

If you have a choice in the matter you will need to think carefully about what suits *you* best. Some people favour **web diagrams** (such as the one on page 24): these people like to plan and record things visually. Other people prefer to **list** what they have done, and what they plan to do, under a series of headings. Thus, for example, the action plan might start with a column that identifies the knowledge, skills or attitudes you are required to demonstrate, and have a second column listing relevant types of evidence. Further columns could show how you went about providing this evidence. You could record:

- how you obtained the information needed;
- the activities undertaken to provide the evidence;
- how you monitored your progress;
- the relevant grading criteria;
- the date when you completed the assignment.

Whatever style you adopt, remember that an action plan needs to show how your plans and thinking have developed as the assignment has progressed. It's not just a snapshot view of the initial planning stage: it's a picture of you in action. It's more like a video recording than a series of 'still' photographs. Action plans are crucial in your assessment because they provide evidence of your ability to take responsibility for your own learning. As you will see below, your growing ability to plan and monitor your own work with less and less assistance from your tutors is a key factor in deciding whether you deserve one of the higher grades.

Remember, too, that the grading criteria provide the central focus for the evidence that you need to gather. That's why it's sensible to record the grading criteria in your action plan. It's easy to lose sight of these if you're not careful. It is for this reason that some colleges and schools design their action plans around the seven grading criteria, so that you are obliged to provide evidence to show how the work you have done meets the relevant grading criteria. In such systems the action plan consists of seven columns, one for each of the grading criteria.

MAKING THE GRADE

As in Chapter 2, we've reached a point where you've been introduced to lots of separate pieces of information which now need to be assembled to show the whole picture. This section offers a completed picture of what you need to achieve by the end of the course in order to be awarded the GNVQ in Health and Social Care. Some pieces of information are drawn from Chapter 2, the rest from this chapter: if any of it is still unclear to you, look back at the relevant section to check what the terms mean and what is involved.

At the end of the GNVQ you could be awarded one of three grades:

- pass;
- merit;
- distinction.

Pass grade

To be awarded a pass grade at Intermediate level you must successfully have completed the following:

- 4 mandatory units;
- 2 optional units;
- 3 core skills units.

To complete a unit successfully you must:

- provide evidence in your portfolio which satisfies all the element requirements;
- provide evidence in the portfolio to show that you have satisfactorily acquired the abilities reflected in the grading criteria;
- pass any externally set tests.

Each unit is assessed separately on completion. A pass grade for a unit is automatic once the three requirements above have been met. The unit can be credited to you should you not complete the whole of the GNVQ.

Merit and distinction grades

To be awarded a merit or distinction grade means doing *better* work, not more work. The decision to award a merit or distinction grade is taken at the end of the GNVQ in the light of your performance throughout the whole of the GNVQ. You will need to show evidence of a higher standard of performance in the achievement of the seven grading criteria, as reflected in the action plans, the assignments and other work presented for final assessment.

The additional evidence that the assessors will be looking for in your portfolio will mainly be evidence of your ability to manage your own learning with progressively less help and guidance from your tutors. In particular, they will want to see evidence of your ability:

- to plan and monitor your own work and performance;
- to explain and justify the decisions you take;
- to assess your own progress and performance, and set your own learning goals;
- to obtain, collect and make use of increasingly complex information;

- to present yourself and your work as would a confident professional.

Because it will take time for you to develop these abilities, those assessing you will look for this additional evidence in the later units in the course.

What this means in terms of each of the grading criteria will be explained to you by your teachers or tutors when they set you an assignment or other activity. The tables reproduced on page 27 will give you an idea of what is involved in achieving a merit or distinction grade for each of the grading criteria. They are taken from an NCVQ publication. Some of the terms used are different from the ones used in this book, so get help if you need to. A word of warning: these tables are liable to change – check with your tutors for the latest version.

TYPES OF ASSESSMENT

Two important points have already been made about the assignments and activities that you will be asked to carry out as part of the GNVQ:

- Assignments and activities are designed to help you to develop the knowledge, skills and attitudes needed to be a successful care worker. They are *not* designed as tests to find out what you do or don't know at particular points in the course.
- Because they are closely linked to the abilities you must develop, they cover a wide range of different types of assessed work.

Let's develop these points a little further.

You may be used to thinking of assessed work as something designed to test what you're already expected to have learned and to know. Most of the assessment in the GNVQ is not like this. The assessed work that you do plays a key role in your development as a professional: the assignments and activities you will be asked to undertake will have been carefully planned to give you practical experience, as well as theoretical knowledge, in the abilities you need to develop.

This is an example of 'learning through doing'. The work that you carry out in the GNVQ is designed to give you opportunities to learn for yourself. As was pointed out in Chapter 2, there are many possible answers to most of the situations a care worker faces. What matters, therefore, is knowing how to apply your knowledge and skills in a professional way. Where this knowledge is factual knowledge – as, for example, in some of the elements in the mandatory units, this will be assessed through the **tests**. The rest of your assessment is designed to help develop your abilities through practice and experience, supported

THE GRADING CRITERIA

Theme 1: Planning

The way the student lays down how s/he will approach and monitor the tasks/activities undertaken during a period of learning.

	merit	distinction
1. Drawing up plans of action	Student independently draws up plans of action for a series of discrete tasks. The plans prioritise the different tasks within the given time period.	Student independently draws up plans for complex activities. The plans prioritise the different tasks within the given time period.
2. Monitoring courses of action	Student independently identifies points at which monitoring is necessary and recognises where revisions to courses of action are necessary. Appropriate revisions to plans are made with guidance from tutor.	Student independently identifies points at which monitoring is necessary and recognises where revisions to courses of action are necessary. Appropriate revisions to plans are made independently.

Theme 2: Information seeking and information handling

The way the student identifies and uses information sources.

	merit	distinction
3. Identifying information needs	Student independently identifies information requirements for a series of discrete tasks.	Student independently identifies the information requirements for complex activities.
4. Identifying and using sources to obtain information	Student independently accesses and collects relevant information for a series of discrete tasks. Student identifies principal sources independently and additional sources are identified by the teacher/tutor.	Student independently accesses and collects relevant information for compex activities. Student uses a range of sources, and justifies their selection.

Theme 3: Evaluation

The way the student retrospectively reviews: the activities undertaken; the decisions taken in the course of that work; alternative courses of action which s/he might have adopted.

	merit	distinction
5. Evaluating outcomes justifying approaches	Student judges outcomes against original criteria for success, justifies the approach used and indicates that alternatives were identified and considered.	Student judges outcomes against original criteria for success and justifies the approach used with a detailed consideration of relevant advantages and disadvantages. Alternatives and improvements are identified.

Theme 4: Quality of outcomes

The way the student synthesises knowledge, skills and understanding; and demonstrates command of the 'language' of the GNVQ area.

	merit	distinction
6. Synthesis	Student's work demonstrates an effective synthesis of knowledge, skills and understanding in response to discrete tasks.	Student's work demonstrates an effective synthesis of knowledge skills and understanding in response to complex activities.
7. Command of 'language'*	Student's work demonstrates an effective command of the 'language' of the GNVQ area at Foundation/Intermediate level[†].	Student's work demonstrates a fluent command of the 'language' of the GNVQ area at Foundation/Intermediate level[†].

*'language' refers to the concepts, forms of expression and presentation used within the GNVQ vocational area or discipline.
[†]Foundation level for Foundation GNVQ students, Intermediate level for Intermediate GNVQ students.

The grading criteria used for awarding merit and distinction grades.
Source: GNVQ: Grading Foundation and Intermediate GNVQs (September 1994)

by help and clear guidance from your tutors, and colleagues in the workplace.

The second point follows from this. Because they are part of the learning process, and closely linked to the abilities you need to develop, the assignments and activities will take different forms. For example, some assignments may concentrate on planning skills, whereas others may focus on particular areas of knowledge about health care practices. Recall the grading criteria within the four GNVQ themes: you will not be expected to show evidence of achieving *each* of the grading criteria *all* of the time. What you can demonstrate will depend on the type of assignment set, and that in turn will depend on what particular skills, knowledge or professional attitudes are being developed within a given unit or element. Each piece of assessed work combines with the other pieces, and together they produce a fully trained care worker.

We now look briefly at some of the main types of assessment used within the GNVQ. On page 15 is a list of the different forms of assessed work which you might use in your portfolio. These could be grouped under the following headings:

- practical exercises;
- written assignments;
- presentations – displays, audio, visual, role-play and simulation;
- timed tasks – written, practical and oral;
- case studies.

Types of assessment are hard to categorise as they often overlap: a case study, for example, may form part of a written assignment or part of a practical exercise.

Practical exercises

Most jobs have practical skills that are important to the outcome and success of the job. Telephonists, for instance, must develop listening and communication skills; secretaries must show competent keyboard and shorthand skills; and care workers must show that they are able to take responsibility for the safety and well-being of those for whom they are caring.

Practical exercises may take place in a special workshop at college or school, or they may be carried out in the workplace. They will involve you, as the carer, demonstrating your ability to carry out a task. This may involve more than one person, or just you alone. Your tutor will observe the exercise, and assess your ability against the action plan you have produced in response to the grading criteria set for the task.

Written assignments

Each **written assignment** you are given will reflect a particular aspect of the course. Your college or school will probably use a set design for assignment work, so that you become familiar with the way tasks are set out. The information you receive will include:

- an introduction, which will give you background information and an overview of the assignment;
- the tasks you are to complete, which will identify the actual work you have to do – a single assignment is usually made up of a number of tasks, which may be written or more practical;
- the grading criteria, which will show you what specific abilities you need to demonstrate in the task or tasks set;
- the core skills involved – in most assignments these will be identified for you, but there will be times when you will be expected to identify them for yourself and show how you used them within the tasks.

Presentations

Presentations are often used as a means of developing and assessing your core skills. For example, you may be asked – or choose – to present evidence of what you have learned by means of mounted displays, audio or visual presentations, role-play, or simulations. (An explanation of simulation is given later in this chapter.) Presentations may be used to support a practical exercise, or you may want to include a written report to demonstrate your learning. Again, the grading criteria involved in this kind of activity will be made clear to you by your tutors.

Timed tasks

Timed tasks allow you to display what you know under specified conditions. You may have to give a talk, to record information, or to use visual aids or practical material to put a point across – in a given amount of time. The task may involve a written piece of work to be completed within a set time. Some tasks may be organised in such a way that you cannot use notes: you will then have to tackle the task using your previous knowledge and experience.

Case studies

Case studies use information about real or imaginary circumstances which you might come across in a caring situation. The studies will have been written by your tutors, and the related tasks will ask you to explore possible lines of action in a given situation. Case studies based on real situations are usually very complicated: your tutors will have modified the information for you so that the task is in keeping with your experience.

FINDING INFORMATION

Whatever type of task you are asked to complete, it will involve you in finding information. This is an important skill which you must acquire; as we've seen, it is one of the grading criteria in Theme 2 of the GNVQ.

You may already be used to getting information from books, but as a health care worker you will need to obtain information from other sources too. In order to do this, you will need communication skills that depend on the spoken word as well as the written word, and you will need to find answers through your own observations as well as through the eyes of others.

This is what we meant earlier by the term *active or independent learning* – taking some of the initiative for your own learning. This requires you to develop some specific skills, such as:

- observing others in action;
- setting up and conducting interviews;
- recording and using oral or spoken information obtained in an interview;
- researching and using information from documentary sources – journals, for instance.

All these skills will become familiar to you as part of the GNVQ, especially through the tasks and assignments you undertake.

PRESENTING YOUR WORK

Let's now consider the practical aspects of presenting your work. Your tutors may have their own views about this, and some schools and colleges may have set procedures to follow.

Effective presentation depends on good personal habits. These need to be learned, not taught! Here are a few of the procedures you may be expected to adopt:

- Try to organise your work so that each task begins on a fresh sheet of paper.
- If **headings** are necessary, supply them.
- If you have access to a **word-processor**, use it; if not, make sure that your **handwriting** is legible. (There is nothing wrong with handwritten work: often it is preferable to poorly word-processed work.)
- Before submitting your work for assessment, check the **spelling**. To avoid errors, use a dictionary as necessary, and, if possible, ask a member of your family or a friend to read your work through for you. If you have word-processed the work, use the 'spell check' before handing in the work.
- Provide a **front cover** for your work. This should clearly state your name, the course, the assignment title, and the name of your teacher or tutor.

- Keep the work together. **Staple** the sheets and, if possible, put the work in a **wallet** so that there is no danger of loose sheets getting lost.
- Provide a **contents page** so that the person assessing the work can see where each section begins and ends.
- Identify and label any illustrations – diagrams, charts or tables.
- Include a **bibliography**, so that the reader knows what books, journals and other materials you have used. Your teachers or tutors will show you how to set out a bibliography.
- If you need to thank people for help you have received, you should include these **acknowledgements** on a separate page near the beginning.
- Refer to any **additional material**, such as leaflets, letters and articles. Explain their relevance to the work you have done so that your tutor is clear why they have been included.
- Always **review** the finished assignment yourself and compare it with your own **standards**. Ask yourself at this stage whether you would be prepared to let a prospective employer see it. Is it a fair and accurate indication of your ability and your commitment?

WHO ASSESSES YOUR WORK?

It is unusual to leave the assessment of your work to one person: you will probably find there are a number of people assessing you. This is to ensure a reliable and unbiased picture of your ability. The **assessors** will probably include:

- school or college staff;
- employers;
- workplace supervisors;
- yourself;
- other students.

A further group of people play a slightly different role. These people are called **verifiers**. It's their job to see that standards are being achieved among all the students in the school or college. They also make sure that all students are being treated fairly and to the same standards. There are two kinds of verifiers:

- internal verifiers;
- external verifiers.

The **internal verifier** will be someone from the staff of the school or college in which you are doing your GNVQ. This person will look at your work on perhaps two occasions a year, for the purposes described above. She or he will not have been involved otherwise in your studies.

The **external verifier** is someone from another college or school who will visit your centre on a number of occasions during the year to make sure that your course is meeting national standards. The external verifier will see a sample of students' work and assess this against standards across the country. If your tutors are uncertain about what final grade to award, they will involve the external verifier in this decision and check it against the national standards.

Internal and external verifiers are keen to meet students and listen to their comments about the course, to find out what they have learned. Be prepared to take part in a constructive discussion with other students and the verifiers.

For the most part, your work will be assessed by your tutors who are responsible for the GNVQ programme. Sometimes employers, too, are involved in assessment, and their contribution can be invaluable. They may also be invited to contribute to a **course review**, in which your views and theirs are considered. It is important that your experiences in the workplace are reflected in the assignments you complete: this is your chance to show that you understand the important relationship between the theoretical knowledge provided in the units and the practical on-the-job experience gained in the workplace.

Occasionally you will be involved with other students in assessing aspects of work on the course. This type of **group assessment** can be very helpful and you will get used to making constructive comments about yourself and others in a group situation. Presenting your work to others can be a little frightening at first but you will be given help with this by your tutors. You will be surprised how quickly you gain confidence in your own ability.

COPING WITH TOO MANY DEMANDS

It's possible at some stage, for whatever reason, that you may find yourself not coping as well as you ought to be doing. This happens to us all at some time in our lives – it's nothing to feel ashamed about.

If it happens to you, the important thing to do is to seek help. Don't think that asking for help is an admission of failure on your part. For example, if you find yourself falling behind with your work, tell your tutors as quickly as possible – they will advise you, or guide you to people who can give you the help you need. You can hand in work at a later date than that specified in the course schedule if there are good reasons for doing so. But no one will know these reasons unless you tell them!

☞ **POINT TO REMEMBER**
Tutors, counsellors and support staff are there to guide and help you with your learning. They want

you to succeed. It's up to you to seek their help when you need to, and to keep them informed about how you feel and how you are coping with the demands of the course.∎

WORK EXPERIENCE

Part of the GNVQ will probably involve you in **work experience** in some aspect of health and social care. You will be prepared for this in college or school by means of practical activities and exercises. These will have been carefully planned to make sure that you know what is expected of you and that you are as ready as you can be for the experiences you will meet at work.

One way of doing this is through classroom **simulation** exercises. These involve putting you into a practical situation which, though it mirrors a real situation, is free from many of the stresses and difficulties you would experience in the actual situation. Simulations allow you to respond to situations, often through **role-play**. You can thereby build knowledge and confidence, so that when you arrive in the workplace you already have a good idea of what to expect.

Through practice of this kind you will develop the ability to cope in the workplace and understand why certain procedures are being carried out. For much of the time in the workplace you will be expected to make observations about what is going on, and to ask questions.

GNVQs involve employers

The workplace **supervisor** will be responsible for reporting on the progress you make. Your tutor will be in touch with your supervisor and will visit the workplace to assess your progress and discuss developments in your learning. Together you should be able to monitor your progress and plan future activities so that your knowledge and experience are constantly being developed.

The time you spend on work placements will also be of value when carrying out assignments related to the GNVQ units. Your own personal, practical experience should always be related to the theoretical knowledge you are acquiring in school or college. How you use your work experience in completing an assignment should form a key part of the action plan for that assignment.

Before you go into the workplace, a number of visits are likely to be arranged for you to experience different care establishments. A tutor may accompany you and the rest of your group, and be available to answer questions and to introduce you to some of the situations in which you may find yourself as a care worker. You will be expected to make observations and to produce a report of the visit. First impressions will be important, but remember that it's easy to get the wrong impression: don't offer opinions that you might later want to change. Always respect the efforts of others, even when you think that you could do better yourself.

Again, you will receive advice from your tutors about how to present a good image of yourself in the workplace.

★★★ REVIEW POINT ★★★

This chapter has provided a great deal of information: it's a lot to take in all at once. Spend a few moments checking that you've taken in what has been said. Look back at the section headings in this chapter, and consider what you need to be sure about at this stage. Make sure, for example, that you can still answer the questions in the 'Review point' on page 24, and especially that you understand about themes, action plans and grading criteria. If you need further help, ask your tutors for guidance.

By now you're probably feeling that you need a break from learning about how the GNVQ works. The next three chapters are about health and social care, and about you taking a more central role in your own learning.

Task: The role of the care worker (page 21)

We are seeking to appoint a care worker who can:

1 tackle problems and find solutions to them;
2 identify the information needed to tackle problems, and know how to go about obtaining it;
3 weigh up the value and relevance of the information obtained;
4 plan work quickly and efficiently, as a member of a team;
5 make decisions, taking into account the time and resources available;
6 produce well-written or spoken reports, care plans, and the like, demonstrating a high level of communication and presentation skills;
7 learn from experience and be prepared to improve upon her or his own practice.

If your list is very different from the one above, ask your tutor to go through yours with you and find out why. If there are abilities above that you have not included in your list, think about them carefully and consider why they are important to a care worker. All of these abilities have to be developed and assessed during your time at college or school if you are to

meet the requirements of the job. Remember, passing the GNVQ should be the same thing as telling an employer that you have the necessary abilities to be a professional care worker.■

Responses to Task: Applying grading criteria (page 25)

Question	GNVQ theme	GNVQ grading criterion
	Process	*Process*
1 How was the route decided upon?	1 Planning	1 Drawing up plans of action
2 Did the original plans work out? If not, why? What was the thinking behind the revised plans?	1 Planning	2 Monitoring courses of action
3 What information was needed to plan the journey?	2 Information seeking and information handling	3 Identifying information needs
4 How was the information obtained? Was this done easily?	2 Information seeking and information handling	4 Identifying and using sources to obtain information
5 How long did the journey take? How long was the journey planned to take?	3 Evaluation	5 Evaluating outcomes and justifying approaches
6 What did the journey cost? Was the cost kept within the planned budget?	3 Evaluation	5 Evaluating outcomes and justifying approaches
7 What was learned in terms of the return journey?	3 Evaluation	5 Evaluating outcomes and justifying approaches
	Outcome	*Outcome*
8 Did those making the journey find it an enjoyable experience? Would they do it again?	4 Quality of outcomes	6 How the piece of work as a whole fits together 7 Use of appropriate communication skills

If your response differs from the one above, discuss your answers with a tutor so that any differences can be explained.

Question 8 may have proved awkward. Judging the quality of an outcome is reasonably straightforward when the outcome is something that has been made or presented, and where definitions of quality are relatively clear and generally agreed. (For instance, most people would agree that a piece of written work should display accurate spelling, correct punctuation and an appropriate use of language and expression.) On the other hand, when the outcomes involved are *not* made or presented, it is often harder to assess their quality. For example, consider outcomes that depend on how we feel towards something, such as a painting, a film or a journey. The result may be a matter of opinion rather than a matter of general agreement, and there may be no rules to guide our decision.

Even so, all outcomes do have qualities that can be assessed, however difficult this might be in practice. Many of the outcomes you will have to achieve as a care worker are very difficult to evaluate in terms of quality, yet high-quality outcomes are still vital aspects of your job! For example, how would we define a good relationship? How would we assess trust and respect? These are things we recognise when we experience them: but this is true, too, for the other people involved. In each case the opinions and feelings of *all* those involved, not just our own, are crucial in assessing the outcome.∎

KEY WORDS AND TECHNICAL TERMS

Action plan The record that shows how you planned and tackled your work. It shows how you approached the task – how much responsibility you took for your own learning and how well you monitored and evaluated your performance.

Evaluation The process by which you review the outcome of your performance at the end of a task and learn from the experience in order to improve your performance next time.

Grade There are three GNVQ grades: pass, merit and distinction. You are awarded a grade at the end of the GNVQ course, when all of your work has been assessed.

Grading criteria These identify the areas of skill and knowledge to be achieved in the GNVQ. They are grouped into four themes.

Monitoring The process by which you review your progress and change your plans where necessary to reflect any new circumstances that may have arisen.

Role-play A situation or drama in which you take the role of one of the characters involved in the action. Role-play allows you to feel what it is like to be in that situation, and so to appreciate how other people may feel and behave in such circumstances.

Simulation An activity specifically designed to imitate a real situation. The roles you play and the decisions you make as the action unfolds should reflect the real situation as closely as possible. Simulations allow you to practise the skills you will need in the real situation.

Themes These provide the framework for the grading criteria against which your work is assessed. There are four themes: planning, information seeking and information handling, evaluation, and quality of outcomes.

Verifiers The people who assess your performance in relation to the course specifications and who maintain the national standards of the GNVQ qualification.

4 • Understanding people

This chapter considers the similar and differing needs of the people you are caring for. You will:

- be made aware that although each individual is unique and special, everyone exists within, and is influenced by, the wider world around them;
- learn to identify and explain some of the factors that make people different;
- look at yourself in terms of your group identity as a student, and see how your own view of yourself differs from the way other people may see you;
- use what you've learned in the previous chapters to help you with the tasks in this chapter;
- continue to develop the ability to think for yourself;
- be introduced, using a story, to a series of 'caring in action' situations for use in the following chapters.

You may by now be feeling that you have spent quite a lot of time on the structure of GNVQ, and relatively little on the things that really interest you – people and caring. The next three chapters will redress the balance. Nevertheless, it is important to realize that you will *never* be in a position to concentrate solely on what you prefer to do. As a care worker in a team, as now while studying on a GNVQ programme, you must know about and work within the broader requirements of the job.

PEOPLE AS INDIVIDUALS

Understanding and dealing with people is a complex activity. We've already stressed the importance of seeing each individual as unique, of recognising each person's *individuality*, and of treating each person as special in their own right. We've acknowledged the importance of establishing relationships with individuals on the basis of trust and confidence, and of valuing and respecting their opinions and feelings. This chapter looks more closely at what is meant by individuality – at *how* each of us is different, not just biologically and physically but in other ways too. Many of these differences will be immediately obvious to you: we have different interests, different

likes and dislikes, and different attitudes and opinions. Just as no two situations are ever exactly alike, so no two people are exactly alike either.

Individual differences

Even though we are all individuals, we do share many things in common. We are all *people*, for example, which gives us a group identity which is different from other living groups such as animals, birds, or plants. Yet we are different from each other in the ways we behave, in the languages that we speak, in the things in which we believe, and in the ways in which we live and organise our lives.

One obvious difference is defined at the moment of conception: eventually we are born either male or female. We thereby become members of a group, men or women, which partly defines our individuality for the rest of our lives. Apart from this difference, and the physical and intellectual characteristics we inherit from our parents, our individuality is primarily determined by the people and things around us – our families, our friends, the groups we join, where we live, the type of job we have, our personal circumstances, and so on. We do not grow up separate from the world we live in: we are part of it.

If you have started your studies in mandatory Unit 2 you will be well aware of the importance of these observations. The work in this section of the book links into your studies in that unit. To have done some work in Unit 2 already will therefore be helpful, though it is not essential. If you are coming to this chapter with no specific knowledge of Unit 2, don't worry: the section that follows this one will provide you with an introduction to the material covered in the unit.

BECOMING A PROFESSIONAL

The focus in this section is still on making you increasingly responsible for your own learning. You need to think for yourself and find out that you are able to take action, confident in the knowledge that you know *what* you are doing, *why* you are doing it, and *how* to do it. These chapters cannot *teach* you how to become a professional: they can only offer you the chance to *learn* for yourself what this involves.

Remember that caring is a practical activity based on a complex mixture of knowledge and skills that have to be used in different situations and with different people. These cannot be taught: as with so much of life, you have to learn which bits of knowledge to apply in which situations, which skills to use and when. You need to learn through the whole activity, by looking at situations and watching people in action, and discovering how to respond through practice and experience.

People in action

The action for your work in this chapter has two parts. The first takes you personally as the subject, and looks at you and *your* individuality from two points of view. It focuses on you as one member of a group of students studying for a GNVQ in Health and Social Care; then it looks at you as an individual within the wider world in which you live.

The second part takes the form of an imaginary situation centring on the lives of some people living in a street on the outskirts of a town. The story, specially written for the purpose, portrays a small group of people at a particular moment in time, going about their daily lives. The story serves as a focus for the material covered in Chapters 5 and 6, which are designed to build on the things you have learned in this chapter by exploring the lives and needs of the people in the story, whose situations may be very different from your own.

Learning through doing

Each of these activities is supported by a range of tasks. As would be the case in real life, some of these you will find relatively straightforward, while others will be more complex.

Two types of task are used. In the first you are asked to identify and consider the factors that shape people's individuality, and use this understanding to help you carry out later activities. You will be expected to make use of the knowledge and skills you have acquired from the previous chapters and from your studies of the GNVQ core skills and the mandatory units, especially Units 2, 3 and 4. The work will include practice in action planning in preparation for your GNVQ assignments.

The second type of task is based on fact-finding. To perform your job efficiently there are certain things you *have* to know which are not matters of personal opinion or judgement. These are factual or technical information, such as information related to people's legal entitlements, to their entitlement to financial assistance, to the range of services and assistance available to people with particular personal needs, and to the sorts of medical conditions you might commonly meet. Knowing these things is crucial to your responsibilities – being a care worker isn't simply a matter of acquiring and demonstrating practical skills. The tests related to the mandatory units, and the GNVQ grading criteria, all require you to provide proof of your factual knowledge.

It would be easier, of course, just to give you the information you need instead of asking you to find it out for yourself. But as a care worker you need to know where to look for information: this is one of the abilities listed in the care worker's job description (page 31). This is reflected in the GNVQ grading criteria for Theme 2: it's your responsibility to provide evidence that you can find the factual information you need. These tasks will help you provide such evidence for your portfolio.

PERCEPTIONS AND PRECONCEPTIONS

Looking at yourself as an individual is a good place to start – presumably you won't be short of information since you know yourself better than anyone else. In this section, then, you will try to identify some of the things that make you the person you are, and the things that make you much the same as some people, but unlike others.

Although you will be asking questions mainly about yourself, many of them will be about you in relation to other people around you. It would help for this activity if you are part of a group of students studying for the GNVQ in Health and Social Care. If this is *not* possible then picture such a group in your mind's eye, and imagine how the other students might respond to the issues you would have shared with them. Since as a care worker you need to be able to put yourself in other people's positions, it's an ability you will do well to develop right from the start.

The task as a whole is divided into three stages. Observations made at the end of each stage will show the purpose and relevance of that part of the activity. Lessons to be learned from the whole exercise are summarised in the 'Points to remember' at the end of the section.

Stage 1: You as a student

IIII➤ TASK *Identifying similarities and differences*
Look at the two questions below. Think about the first question by yourself, and the second in discussion with the other members of your group.

- In what ways does being a student make me the *same* as other members of the group?
- In what ways, as a student, am I *different* from other members of the group?

If you need some starting points for the second question, try the following:

- Are we all doing the GNVQ course for the same reasons?
- Do we all like being a student?
- Are we all roughly the same age?
- Do we all dress alike?
- Do we all behave alike?
- Do we all work as hard as each other?
- Do we all belong to the same school or college social clubs or organisations?
- Do we all have the same interests?
- Do we all speak with the same accent?∎

OBSERVATIONS

In answer to the first question, you probably noted that being a student meant that certain aspects of your lives were alike or very similar. You all attend the same school or college, for instance. You are all doing the same GNVQ course; you attend the same classes and lectures much of the time; you observe the same regulations while in school or college; and as a group you share many facilities that are not open to those outside the school or college. In all sorts of ways, therefore, your experience as a student affects your life and your personal identity at the moment.

What about the differences? Probably you found that you are all doing the GNVQ in Health and Social Care for different reasons. You won't all share the same attitudes towards school or college, or towards your work and studies. It's unlikely that you have all been achieving the same grades for your work, or that you all enjoy the same activities.

Within any group of people, then, your sense of identity is partly defined by a number of shared characteristics and expectations. On the other hand, as individuals you remain a collection of very different people. Having a particular role – in this case, being a student – gives you part of your individuality, but only part of it.∎

Stage 2: Other people's perception of you

As a student you have a certain group identity which people outside the group would recognise. We each have a picture in our mind of what being 'a student' means. This is our **perception**: our view of the world, how we see things.

But just as we have views about things, so other people have views about these things – and they may be different. This is especially true for group

identities: those inside a particular group often see themselves in one way, while those outside may see them very differently.

▷ TASK Identifying group identities

Imagine that a national survey is being conducted about people's perceptions of students. You have been asked to take part, as have a number of people from the general public in your local area.

One of the items for response in the survey is:

- List the *six* general characteristics which in your opinion best describe a typical student.

Spend about 15 minutes discussing your response with the other members of your group. At the end of this time, agree a list of the six characteristics which you all believe best describe your group identity – how you see yourselves.

Now compare your list with the one provided on page 37, the response of a member of the public.∎

OBSERVATIONS

If your list matched the one on page 37, then the exercise failed! But probably the two lists were very different, and the response on page 37 may even have annoyed you. Probably you found at least three of this person's perceptions unacceptable:

- It is not factually accurate to say that all students are young.
- Some of the perceptions refer to a small section only of the group. They are not wholly accurate: rather they are prejudiced and biased.
- The list may not accurately reflect you personally.

A typical student?

All too often, of course, we make personal judgements about people and the things around us on the basis of our general *preconceptions* about them. This is not a helpful way of seeing things, and certainly it is a poor basis for establishing good relationships with people. (We shall have more to say about this in Chapters 5 and 6.)∎

Stage 3: You as an individual

We observed in Stage 1 that the individuals within your group are likely to be different from other members in many ways. Some of you, for example, may have chosen to do a GNVQ in Health and Social Care because it has always been an ambition to work with people in need; others may be doing it because their parents or teachers suggested it. Whatever the reasons, we can be certain that the decision will have been influenced by a range of people and a range of experiences in your life so far. The same is likely to be true for all the other characteristics you identified as making you different from members of the group. There are many features of your individuality which you will have brought with you to school or college, and which your experiences at school or college will have helped to shape and extend.

What are the key factors in our lives which help to make us who we are, which influence the decisions we make, and which affect the way we feel and the way we see ourselves and others? Often we are too close to be the best judges of ourselves. Nevertheless it's important that we understand ourselves before we take on the responsibility of making decisions about the lives of others.

Let's try now to see what factors in particular have made you into the person you are – or the person you think you are! Again, this task has two parts, the first to be completed on your own, and the second to be discussed with the group.

 TASK *Identifying factors that have influenced you*

Go back to the profile you constructed in Stage 1, which identifies some of the differences between yourself and other members of the group. From these, select what you think are the three most significant differences. You may, for example, feel that you work harder than most of the others, or that you enjoy different social activities, or that you have a particular interest that is not shared by the others. You may have a different religious belief, speak with a different accent, or have a particular political point of view. Whatever they are, pick the three most significant ones.

Take each of these aspects in turn. For each, try to identify any particular reasons which you think might help explain this aspect of your individuality.

When you've done this, find two or three members of your group who you think are least like yourself. Share your findings with them. (The idea behind working with people *unlike* yourself is that this sometimes enables you to see more clearly what lies behind your own attitudes, beliefs, behaviour, interests and other personal characteristics.)∎

OBSERVATIONS

Whatever characteristics you chose, and whatever factors you identified to explain these characteristics, you probably found that one factor emerged as more influential than the rest – the influence of your family, or those responsible for your upbringing. In all kinds of ways your home, and the life around it, will have had a powerful effect in making you the person you are today. Perhaps it was a member of your family who advised you to study for a GNVQ in Health and Social Care, or perhaps your choice of career was influenced by the fact that you have a parent or close friend whose job is in caring.

As individuals we also belong to families, and families in turn are defined or grouped according to further factors, such as class, race, wealth or religion. If you have studied mandatory Unit 2 you will already know something about these factors, and how they affect people's individuality and well-being. In the next chapter we shall look more closely at some of them.∎

POINTS TO REMEMBER

Though you've concentrated on yourself so far, what you have learned about understanding yourself applies just as much to understanding others.

There are five points to remember. Think carefully about each of them, referring back if necessary to the activities you have just undertaken. Begin to consider how each of the points might apply to people other than yourself, to people you don't know, and particularly to people whose circumstances may be very different from yours. Some of the points below have been deliberately developed to help you think beyond the examples used so far.

1 *People differ* Understanding people is a complex business because as individuals we are all different.
2 *People belong to groups* Each individual will belong to a number of different groupings during his or her life. Some of these groupings will be defined at conception: gender, colour of eyes and skin, for example. Some will reflect personal circumstances: being employed or unemployed; being an unskilled, skilled or professional worker; being a student, a pensioner (senior citizen), and so on. Others will reflect personal choices: clubs joined, a team supported, the circle of close friends kept, the church belonged to, and so forth.

3 *People share group identities* Groups of people share a group identity which emphasises the characteristics they have in common. Thus, as a student you share with your fellow students a number of common features and expectations in this part of your lives. The same is true for other groups – those who are British, those who are unemployed, the members of a band, the members of a local environmental group, and so on.

4 *People have different perceptions* Those who belong to particular groupings often see themselves differently from those outside these groupings. Thus, as a student you may be aware that other people perceive you in a way that you feel is not an accurate reflection of you as an individual. Such perceptions can be very hurtful, perhaps especially when people have no choice about belonging to the particular group – for example, a group of people of a given age, or with skin of a given colour.

5 *People are particularly influenced by families* Each person's individuality develops from a wide range of experiences and influences which accumulate throughout their lives. The family plays a particularly significant part in shaping each person's early identity. But the family in its turn (and therefore the individuals within it) belongs to other groupings according to class, wealth, religion, and race.∎

 Task: Identifying group identities (page 35)

Below are the six features that made up one member of the public's perception of typical students:

- young and often immature;
- scruffy and untidy;
- lazy and disorganised;
- supporters of causes that they know nothing about and have no experience of;
- irresponsible with money;
- against authority whenever possible.

KEY WORDS AND TECHNICAL TERMS

Accent A particular form of pronunciation, or way of speaking, which varies between individuals, localities and regions of the country. For example, Geordie is an accent common amongst many people living in and around Newcastle upon Tyne; Cockney is an accent found amongst many Londoners.

Class One of the different social groupings that people may be classified as belonging to, such as the working class, the middle class or the upper class. These classifications are largely based on the occupation or job of the person or family concerned.

Community centre A place provided within the community for recreation and leisure activities.

The public perception of a student?

Conception The point of fertilisation when the female's ovum, or egg, unites with the male's sperm. Conception may result in pregnancy and the development of a new individual.

Gender The role associated with being male or female. Sex defines the biological state of being either male or female; gender identifies the roles and behaviours linked to these.

Group identity Because groups of people have certain things that they all share in common, these shared characteristics tend to define how the group is seen. Thus families usually share a common name and a house, for example, and have an obvious group identity. Supporting a certain football team or pop group can also create a recognisable group identity.

Hypertension Abnormally high blood pressure. People like Bob, who has high blood pressure, will have an increased risk of suffering a stroke.

Individuality A person's own character and personality: what makes him or her different from everyone else.

Legal entitlement Something that you have the right to by law. In terms of health and social welfare, this refers to the legal right to receive certain state benefits, such as a pension if you are a senior citizen, or social security if you are unemployed.

Meals on wheels A service delivering hot midday meals to elderly people in their own homes. This service is the responsibility of the local authority, but deliveries are usually carried out by volunteers.

Paediatrician A doctor who specialises in the treatment of children and their diseases.

Perception An idea or opinion we form about something (or someone) before we have any first-hand experiences of them.

Profile A brief description of something or somebody. By identifying some of your characteristics as a student and as a person, you constructed a profile of yourself.

Race A group of people who trace their origins or ancestry to a common source. Thus, the English are a race of people whose origins are different from those of the Scots or Welsh. Today Britain is made up of people of a variety of different races, each with its own origin and background.

Redundancy The position you are in when you lose your job because there is no longer any work available in the job you were doing. When businesses or factories are closed down because they are no longer needed, the people working in them are made redundant.

Social services A department within a local authority, responsible for providing a range of social care services for those in need. These services are described in Chapter 7.

Watching other people in action

So far we've concentrated on you and your individuality, what makes you the person you are. But caring is *about* other people and their needs, about understanding the factors and circumstances that affect other people's lives and their well-being. Understanding yourself may seem easy in comparison, but that's only because you already know most of the answers. The questions you need to ask are much the same whoever you are trying to understand, or whatever situation you are trying to make sense of: it's the answers that are different.

Looking at and understanding the lives and needs of others will provide the focus for the rest of this chapter and the chapters that follow. They will take as their basis our second piece of action, an imaginary portrayal of the lives of a group of people living in a street on the outskirts of a large town. The people in the story are portrayed as real people, with real names, and surrounded by real issues, problems and needs, but they are all fictitious. Although this is a story, we want the characters and the action to be as realistic as possible.

Read the story through once, quickly. As there are a lot of people involved and a lot of detail to remember, it may be helpful then to glance at the illustrations. These identify the characters in the story and tell us something about them. There is also an illustration of the street in which most of the action takes place. This should remind you that visual images can be used to illustrate the written word. It

ought also to alert you to the dangers of relying on your own perceptions of other people and other situations: it's often helpful to try to picture situations, as you think they might be from your own knowledge and experience, but remember that those involved may see things differently. You must always be prepared to alter your perception of things when you realise that people or situations are not as you imagined them to be.

Read the story through a second time and begin to take notice of what is happening to the main characters. In what ways is the action relevant to you as a care worker? Again, try to see the characters in your mind's eye, and relate them to people and situations from your own experience. Remember that each individual is special in their own right; each has particular needs.

The people from the story will be used in the next two chapters to help you with:

- finding explanations for the ways people behave in different situations and circumstances;
- tasks which try to find practical solutions to meet the needs of the characters described;
- linking your learning to the GNVQ mandatory, core skills and optional units, and to the GNVQ assessment themes and grading criteria.

You may wish to have your dictionary handy so that you can look up the meanings of any words or technical terms you're not familiar with, and also a file in which to note down things that you feel are significant as you read the story.

A day in Hotspur Street

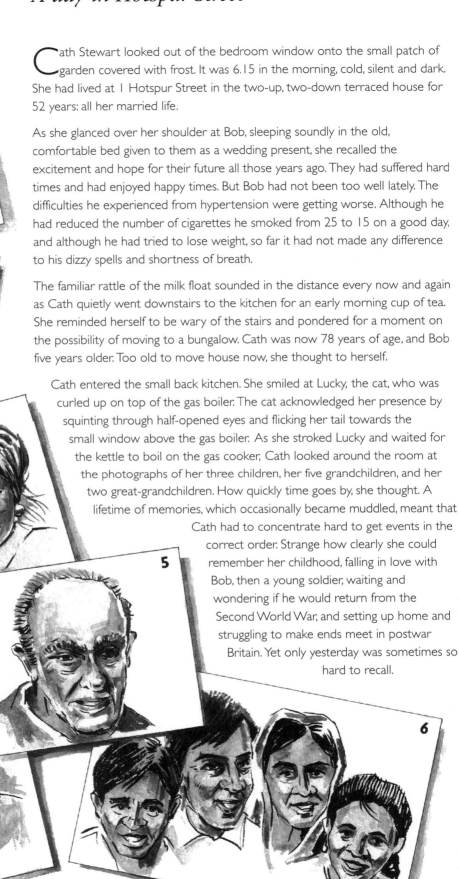

Cath Stewart looked out of the bedroom window onto the small patch of garden covered with frost. It was 6.15 in the morning, cold, silent and dark. She had lived at 1 Hotspur Street in the two-up, two-down terraced house for 52 years: all her married life.

As she glanced over her shoulder at Bob, sleeping soundly in the old, comfortable bed given to them as a wedding present, she recalled the excitement and hope for their future all those years ago. They had suffered hard times and had enjoyed happy times. But Bob had not been too well lately. The difficulties he experienced from hypertension were getting worse. Although he had reduced the number of cigarettes he smoked from 25 to 15 on a good day, and although he had tried to lose weight, so far it had not made any difference to his dizzy spells and shortness of breath.

The familiar rattle of the milk float sounded in the distance every now and again as Cath quietly went downstairs to the kitchen for an early morning cup of tea. She reminded herself to be wary of the stairs and pondered for a moment on the possibility of moving to a bungalow. Cath was now 78 years of age, and Bob five years older. Too old to move house now, she thought to herself.

Cath entered the small back kitchen. She smiled at Lucky, the cat, who was curled up on top of the gas boiler. The cat acknowledged her presence by squinting through half-opened eyes and flicking her tail towards the small window above the gas boiler. As she stroked Lucky and waited for the kettle to boil on the gas cooker, Cath looked around the room at the photographs of her three children, her five grandchildren, and her two great-grandchildren. How quickly time goes by, she thought. A lifetime of memories, which occasionally became muddled, meant that Cath had to concentrate hard to get events in the correct order. Strange how clearly she could remember her childhood, falling in love with Bob, then a young soldier, waiting and wondering if he would return from the Second World War, and setting up home and struggling to make ends meet in postwar Britain. Yet only yesterday was sometimes so hard to recall.

1: Cath and Bob at No. 1   2: Tom on his wedding day
3: Lisa and her mother at No. 5   4: Jenny, Dave, Zoë, Stephen and Nick at No. 3
5: Jack the milkman at No. 7   6: Yasmin and Abdul Azir with Rani and Syed

Hotspur Street

Cath with Lucky the cat

The whistle from the kettle as the water boiled disturbed her thoughts – she had never wanted to use that gleaming electric contraption in the cupboard under the sink – and as her shaking hand removed it, she heard a baby's muffled crying through the wall.

Next door Jenny was trying to force her weary body, comfortably tucked under the warm duvet, to brave the sharp winter air of morning. How she wished the central heating boiler had been repaired. The spare part was going to cost £90.00, and although the landlord had reassured her that he was arranging for it to be repaired, she was still waiting for a visit from the men from British Gas. She wished that she could arrange for the repairs to be carried out herself, but Dave had been out of work for three months, and with the new baby coming along she had had to give up her part-time evening job at the supermarket. It was a struggle to manage with hardly any money coming in. Another sharp hunger cry interrupted Jenny's thoughts as she struggled into her dressing gown.

She felt her way towards the other side of the bedroom in the dim morning light, noticing that Dave slept on undisturbed, and wondered if their luck would change soon. Shivering, she lifted Zoë out of her cot, gave her a kiss, and marvelled at the strength of the tiny eight-week-old body as it strained in search of milk. The young mother felt the silent morning wrap around her and was grateful that Zoë's crying had not disturbed Stephen and Nick, asleep in the other bedroom.

Outside in the narrow road Jack was carefully negotiating the battery-operated milk float around the icy patches. The bottles of milk glistened with cold and the eggs, butter, orange juice and yoghurt were in danger of freezing. Jack knew this neighbourhood well. He had been born 62 years ago at No. 7. There was a time when he knew every person in the street by name, their consumption of milk, and what was going on in their lives. In fact, when he took over the milk round from his father 37 years ago, it was an old cart horse called Linden that had pulled the float. He remembered the excitement as a child

Zoë's early morning feed

when he and his friends would run alongside Linden and bring treats for him, and how Tom was always ready with his shovel to collect the horse droppings for his beloved rose bushes.

Jack was startled out of his peaceful daydreaming by the angry shouting of the very man he was thinking about. There was Tom, an old man now and unable to keep at bay the weeds that had long ago strangled the roses he had tended so lovingly. Tom was agitated. Jack made his way across the slippery road to the old man, who stood on the cold step. As he approached, Tom waved his spindly arm and stamped his slippered feet with all his strength.

'They've been at it all night,' he yelled breathlessly. 'I can't get them to go to bed.'

Jack took a deep breath and wondered how long this could go on. Tom's behaviour had been unpredictable for some time, in fact ever since Mildred, his only daughter, had died suddenly two months ago.

'Now then, what's the problem today?' Jack enquired as he guided the old man off the cold step and into the house.

Jenny could hear the commotion in the street and wondered if it was Tom. She remembered happier times for the old man, when Mildred was alive. She had cared for him and protected him. In fact Mildred was sadly missed by many

people. She was one of those reliable people who always seemed to know the answer if there was a problem. When Gladys Adams' granddaughter Jane came on holiday in the summer, she could not have managed without Mildred. Jane came to stay with her grandmother every year during the school holidays because her mother was a single parent who could not afford to take time off work.

Jane had been born with a disorder called Down's syndrome, and one day Gladys had taken her to the park and she had fallen off the slide and broken her leg. Jane stayed with Gladys for six weeks, and during this time Mildred organised the loan of a wheelchair from the Red Cross, borrowed toys from the toy library in town and called in to read to Jane almost every day. When Jenny, Dave and the boys moved into the rented house on the opposite side of the street last year, Mildred was the first person to come over and welcome them. She took such an interest in them all and the children adored her.

How sad, Jenny thought, to die so young. Mildred had looked after her father for many years and appeared to be in such good health, and so robust. She died in her sleep of a heart attack two days before Zoë was born. No one could be sure whether Tom even remembered now exactly who Mildred was.

Abdul Azir also heard the disturbance as he fed the birds in the back yard in the house next to Tom's. He opened the back door, calling at the same time to Yasmin, who was preparing breakfast, that he was going next door.

Jack was relieved to see Abdul, not only because he was concerned about leaving the milk float unattended but also because he was way behind schedule and some people got cross when their milk was delivered late.

'Leave him to me,' Abdul said. Jack gave his thanks, saying that he would see Abdul later, and went on his way.

Tom was more confused than usual. He thought there were other people in the house causing a disturbance. Abdul tried to reassure him that there was no one else in the house and that the noise was imaginary, but it did no good. Tom had obviously been to bed because he was still in his pyjamas and slippers, but as Abdul looked around the living room he wondered how long Yasmin, Cath, Bob, Jack and he could go on coping with the situation. Every drawer and cupboard in the room had been emptied out onto the floor. Cutlery, crockery, clothes, old letters, books and pens were strewn around. The hearth was littered with bits of food, cigarette ends, bottles and packs of tablets, and other debris.

'Calm down Tom,' Abdul soothed as he put a jumper around the old man's shivering body. 'I want them out,' shouted Tom. 'They are after me and I can't get away from them. Look, there goes that boy with my pillow.'

Abdul was at a loss; he had never seen Tom so agitated. He was pulling at his clothes and looking around with eyes that stared at imaginary people and objects. When Yasmin arrived at Tom's back door she entered calling softly, 'Here's a nice cup of tea and some toast.' This had a calming effect on Tom and he became engrossed in dipping the toast into the tea and chewing on it with his toothless gums. The couple looked at each other over Tom's head and said nothing. Incidents like this were not new. During the past eight weeks Tom had changed a great deal. Often he did not know what time of day it was, nor indeed what day of the week it was. His appearance was unkempt and dishevelled. Some days he knew his neighbours, on others he struggled to remember their names. Indeed, there had been an occasion when he had not known where he was.

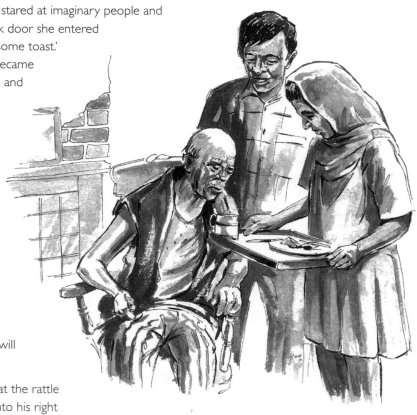

'You get off to work, Abdul,' Yasmin said. 'I will stay here for a while.'

Meanwhile, back at No. 1 Bob had stirred at the rattle of the milk bottles. He tried to roll over onto his right side but nothing happened. He lay very still; only his eyes moved as he looked at the chinks of light peeping through the drawn curtains. Take some slow deep breaths, he told himself. Remember Dr Smart's advice: keep calm. Bob wanted to shout out for Cath to come. He tried to regulate his breathing but it was impossible. He tried to call out but no sound came. Sweat lay cold upon his forehead. He couldn't move. His body felt numb and his mind was unable to focus on what was happening. Bob drifted into unconsciousness.

Downstairs Cath was sitting at the kitchen table, enjoying her cup of tea and unaware of Bob's crisis upstairs. She was writing a shopping list and planning the day in her mind; first get dressed and make breakfast. Bob and Cath always began the day with porridge and toast and listened to the news on the radio. Strange how the habits of a lifetime could give a sense of security and well-being. Then do the shopping, call in at the library to renew that thriller Bob was reading, and call in on Tom over the road to make sure that he was ready with the money when the meals-on-wheels volunteer brought his dinner.

'No more daydreaming, time to get the day going,' she said out loud to Lucky, giving the cat's ear a tweak. As Cath began the slow climb up the stairs she wondered why she could not hear the radio. Before getting dressed Bob always lay in bed, listening to the weather forecast. Anyway, a lie-in would do him good; he deserved to take life a little easier after all those years working.

As soon as Cath entered the bedroom she knew instinctively there was something wrong. She registered the still shape of Bob's body under the covers, and her heart began to race as she gasped for breath and felt a cold shiver of fear tingle down her back. She tried to rouse Bob's lifeless body, calling his name and shaking his shoulder, but there was no response. She ran her hand across his cheek and the skin felt cold and clammy. Help, I must get help. Thoughts raced through her head. Has Bob had a stroke because of the hypertension? Should I stay with him? Open the window, shout out? Go to Yasmin over the road and ring Dr Smart? Should I go to Lisa at No. 5? If only we had a telephone.

Lisa was surprised when she heard the banging on the door so early in the morning. She had just emerged from a hot shower, and was about to get dressed and hurry off to work at the nursing home. It can't be the post at this time, she thought, it's far too early. On opening the door she was startled to see Cath in such a distressed state: she was deathly white, her hands and lips were shaking, and she was stuttering words about Bob dying upstairs and her not knowing. Lisa moved quickly, wrapping her dressing gown tightly around her as she strode ahead of Cath to the open door of No. 1.

She ran up the stairs two at a time and entered the front bedroom. She worked instinctively. Check for a pulse. Check for obstructions. Is Bob breathing? Yes, he is. Relieved, she slipped the pillows out from under his head and gently eased his right arm forward so that he lay in the recovery position. Hearing Cath entering the house, she ran to the top of the stairs to give her the good news that Bob was alive and to stop her coming upstairs. Lisa went halfway down the staircase and leaned over the banister: gently she instructed Cath to go back to No. 5 and ask her mother to ring for an ambulance. Then, squeezing her hand, she reassured her that everything would be all right.

It was some time before Lisa could focus on the start to her day. Cath had gone off to hospital in the ambulance with Bob, who was still unconscious and blue around the mouth, but alive. She was going to be very late for work, but felt thankful that her Mum had phoned The Gables to let them know what had happened. At least they know I will get there as soon as I can, she thought. She was aware of the difficulties caused when staff did not ring in and simply didn't turn up, and the strain this put on everyone else. She was glad to be back in her own bedroom for a few minutes, to get over the shock of seeing Bob lying so still, of thinking that he might be dead, and how she would break the news to Cath. She smiled to herself as she remembered the way her mind had worked. So many conflicting thoughts, yet the actions she carried out had been precise and followed a pattern and would, she hoped, contribute to saving Bob's life.

Lisa's thoughts were broken when her mother entered her bedroom carrying a tray with fresh tea and toast on it. 'Into bed for breakfast,' she instructed her daughter. 'Oh no,' wailed Lisa, 'I'm late for work as it is!' Lisa's mother put the tray on the chest of drawers and put her arms around Lisa. 'I am so proud of you, and so is Mrs Hall at The Gables. She wants you to take your time and go into work when you feel ready.'

Lisa was relieved to hear this. Complying with her mother's wishes, she climbed into bed. She thoroughly enjoyed her breakfast in bed, alongside the discussion with her mother about the difficulties of growing old and coping with ill health. Lisa had always wanted to work as a nursing assistant, and had been lucky enough to be offered the job at The Gables after being on a student placement there last year. She loved the work, but knew she wanted to go back to college to improve her academic qualifications next year so that eventually she could become a social worker. Her boyfriend Geoff had followed the same caring course last year, but he had decided to stay on at college for another two years, to get a qualification which would enable him to study to become a psychiatric nurse. Lisa sighed and acknowledged to her mother that she had needed the rest and reflection on the morning's hectic start. Now, though, she felt fine to get up and go off to work.

Jenny had heard the ambulance come wailing into the street and stop at Cath and Bob's. What now? she wondered. Dave refused to be disturbed, and did not respond to her request to go along and offer help. It was odd from the man who only six months before had raised £100 for the local hospice in the works' fun run, from the man who used to play football and darts, and who had organised a collection of gifts for Children in Need from the playgroup Nick went to. How their lives had changed since that awful Friday when Dave had returned home with his final pay packet unopened and a redundancy letter.

Jenny had watched the changes in Dave's behaviour over the last few weeks and felt powerless to help. He rarely got up before midday. He hardly went out any more. He was short-tempered with the children if they made a noise and rarely acknowledged Zoë's existence. Jenny could feel the warm tears beginning to trickle over her cheeks. Never in her whole life had she felt so alone. She had left the maternity unit 24 hours after Zoë had been born and now knew that this had been too soon. She was also letting the present situation get in the way of attending her postnatal check-up.

If only everything had happened the way I planned it, she whispered to Zoë, stifling a cry of despair into the baby's blanket. Her sister had felt dreadful about not being able to keep her promise and come to stay after the baby was born. She had known how tired and lonely Jenny would be. They had always been close, but more so since their parents had died two years ago.

Jenny's thoughts were shattered by the sound of two wailing sirens rushing along the landing to greet her. Steve and Nick were pretending to be police cars chasing robbers. As they rolled onto the floor at her feet, laughing at their own game, she too smiled. She put Zoë back into her cot before chasing the boys along the landing, down the stairs, through the kitchen and into the bathroom. Stephen was six, Nick two years younger; Jenny certainly had her work cut out. The boys did not seem to feel the cold. Their skinny bodies darted about the bathroom, cleaning teeth, washing hands and faces, and pulling on clothes. Nick tried hard to keep up with his older brother. His chubby fingers struggled with the laces on his shoes, while Nick proudly and deftly tied his and ran into the kitchen shouting 'Slowcoach!' at his brother.

'You leave him alone,' his mother retorted. 'He does very well for his age.' Nick burst through the door crying with frustration and anger. Jenny tried to calm the child, but he was unable to understand why he couldn't be just like his brother. Jenny could hear the baby crying upstairs and distracted Nick by asking him to get the cereal out of the cupboard and put it on the table. While he was busy she asked Stephen to come upstairs with her. Zoë beamed at the sight of Stephen's face peering into hers as he mimicked baby noises. 'Carry the changing bag downstairs, Steve,' Jenny instructed as she lifted Zoë out of her cot, and together they made their way back to the kitchen.

Jenny hurried about giving the boys cereal and toast. She felt cross that Dave was lying in bed, showing no interest in the events of the morning and seemingly unaware of how much there was to do each day with three small children to care for. She did not want another unpleasant scene in front of the children, however, so she had to contain her anger. At least the kitchen was cosy from the heat of the oven. The oven gave off plenty of warmth, and although the cost was a worry she had to keep them warm. With a sigh she said, 'Right, let's get going.' With that the boys started to tuck Zoë into her pram and edge it through the narrow doorway into the hall, towards the front door.

Stephen burst out into the cold morning, pulling his anorak on, and Nick took hold of his mother's hand. 'I hate playgroup,' he sobbed. 'I want to stay at home.' Inwardly, Jenny groaned. Please don't let this happen, she thought, not this morning. Nick had always been hesitant about new things, and rather clingy compared with Stephen. She ignored the little voice as it repeated its request, and hurried them along the slippery path towards Hartop Primary School. As soon as Nick was handed to her wrapped in the hospital sheet Jenny had known that there was something wrong. He looked strange to her. He was so small and still. She was reassured by the staff that he was all right but it was not long after the delivery that the paediatrician came to tell her and Dave that Nick was to have some tests. After days of worry they were told that there was nothing physically wrong with the baby, but his reflexes and reactions were slow.

Jenny only had Stephen to compare Nick with, but she could see clearly that the second baby was very different from the first. Stephen had come into the world in a rage, and been robust and strong from the start. But Nick was small and sensitive to loud noises or play that was too rough. That was part of the problem. Jenny knew there was a group of boys at playschool who enjoyed the rough and tumble of boisterous play: Nick just didn't like it. It was the same at home. If Steve was on his own with Nick they would play happily for hours, but if one of his playmates joined in, Nick usually ended up crying and feeling hurt and left out.

When the bedraggled little family arrived at the school entrance, Steve was happy to run off through the door without a backward glance in response to the goodbyes from his mother and brother. Jenny tightened the belt on her mac and lifted Nick onto the foot of the pram. He sat quietly for a few minutes sucking his thumb, then sobbed quietly to himself. 'I don't like playgroup.' Jenny could feel the pain of sadness in her heart. She wanted him to go. She treasured the time alone with Zoë and she got such a lot done in the house. She felt unsure of herself and had been in this position before with Nick clinging onto her and Mrs Robertson encouraging him into the Community Centre.

Jenny had been assured in the past by the playgroup leader that Nick would settle down and enjoy the activities once she had gone. But on each occasion that Nick had been distressed, Jenny had collected him promptly at 12 o'clock only to find a subdued, attention-seeking and weepy child. As she looked down at Nick snuggling into the pram covers she did not know what to do, and felt very lonely and a little afraid.

Dr Smart's car drew up outside Tom's house at 9.05. Yasmin opened the door and welcomed Fay into the house. The two women smiled at each other in the knowing way that says, 'Well, here we are again.' They both knew that circumstances were leading towards a crisis. Tom could not continue to live alone, putting himself at risk and relying on his neighbours for care. Fay asked Tom how he was feeling. 'Never felt better,' was the gruff reply. The early morning disturbances were long forgotten. Fay prescribed more sedation and asked Yasmin if she could make sure that he took two tablets before going to bed. Yasmin agreed, but once more wondered how long she could cope with the burden of looking after someone as demanding as Tom. He had no living relatives who could handle his affairs for him, and all he possessed in the world was the little terraced house. The community nurse from the Health Centre had called every other day since Mildred's death, but Tom was calm and rarely agitated then.

The changes in Tom's behaviour had developed gradually over the last five weeks or so, and although Dr Smart had requested that a social worker visit and assess Tom's needs, nothing had happened. She made a mental note to ring the local office but knew how busy and short of time everyone was at Social Services. She knew that she was powerless to solve Tom's problems until the situation had become desperate. She also knew that she had a long list of home visits, a surgery that would run late, and a baby clinic to fit into her working day. On the way out of the house she turned and asked Yasmin how her children, Rani and Syed, were. Yasmin hesitated. 'Fine, we are all getting along much better.' How far from the truth, Yasmin thought to herself as she waved goodbye to the doctor.

Rani was threatening to leave home and not continue her studies, and Syed was rebelling against family values and society in general. How easy it had been when they were younger. Then they had accepted and respected the traditions of their parents' homeland and, at the same time had fitted into a culture very different from their own. She wanted the children to be happy but found it difficult to understand why there was such conflict. Yasmin went back into Tom's living room where he was sleeping peacefully in the chair. She removed the tea cup and tidied up the kitchen before leaving quietly and returning to her own home.

Jack had made it safely back to the depot with the milk float, and now he set off up the hill back to Hotspur Street. Although the sun shone brightly there was no warmth from it: the frost was not going to thaw. A harsh, cold winter was forecast and today was the beginning of it, he thought. He pulled his coat tightly around him.

Another day done – for Jack

5 • Identifying and assessing needs: older people

This chapter continues to explore the theme of understanding people and their needs. In this chapter you will:

- be introduced to some of the skills, knowledge and procedures involved in identifying and assessing individual need;
- be helped, through the story, to understand how people's (especially older people's) personal circumstances are an important factor when identifying and assessing needs;
- acquire some basic information about the nature of older people's entitlements to support;
- make use of the knowledge acquired in the GNVQ mandatory Units 1, 2, 3 and 4;
- be provided with opportunities to gather evidence related to the Theme 2 grading criteria in the GNVQ assessment.

This chapter focuses mainly on the older people in the story. There are several reasons for this. Firstly, since older members of the population experience a variety of needs, many of which are relatively easy to recognise, they offer a good starting-point for your training in the processes of identifying and assessing needs. However, there is a danger in this: it may suggest that older people are a readily identifiable group, with very similar and predictable needs and characteristics. This provides a second reason for the choice: this study offers an opportunity to identify and challenge some of the negative attitudes that are often held about older people. Finally, the choice makes sense because you, a future care worker, can expect to spend a substantial proportion of your professional life caring for older people.

Do remember that the individuals you met in the story are imaginary. Some of them may have appeared somewhat larger than life, and perhaps life is seldom quite as dramatic as described in the story. Nevertheless, it provided us with a snapshot of a variety of human situations which are all too real for a great many people, at some stage of their lives.

PEOPLE IN NEED

The people in Hotspur Street seem to be experiencing their fair share of difficulties, some greater than others, and some more obvious than others.

Identifying who needs what, and when, is not a straightforward matter. Some people enjoy the benefit of extensive support, while others experience less support; some have more time to lend others a hand, others have less. Noticeably, the causes of some people's needs appear very similar, yet the help they require is different. Both Bob and Tom, for instance, are experiencing health and social problems, yet Tom's appear more serious than Bob's: this is because Bob's personal circumstances are different – he has a wife, Cath, to support him, whereas Tom hasn't. We need to treat each individual as special, and to remember that there are many factors that may make one person's situation better or worse than another's. Identifying and assessing need is about making such judgements.

Dave and his family also have needs, which are both similar to, and yet different from, Bob's and Tom's. They are *similar* in so far as they have been brought about by a sudden change in their personal circumstances. But they are *different* in that they are economic, rather than medical; they are also different in that they affect more people; and they are different again in so far as Dave and his family are of an age such that they may be better able to cope with their problems, and ultimately to solve them. Even so, the needs are no less significant to the individuals concerned at that moment in time.

Jane's situation also is different. Her needs are not the result of any sudden changes to her fitness or lifestyle. Her physical and mental problems are **congenital:** she has had them since birth. Nor can she expect to experience any marked improvement in her condition for the rest of her life, which means that she will have to learn to cope with it as best she can, with the support available to her.

Different people have different needs

On the surface, then, we are aware of a number of people whose immediate needs are fairly easy to identify from what we can see of their circumstances. Below the surface, however, there are likely to be others who also have needs, but whose problems, for one reason or another, are less easy to spot. This may be because the circumstances involved are less problematic or less obvious, or because some people are simply better at coping with things than others. Yasmin appears to fall into this category.

Many people we meet are getting on with their lives without any apparent difficulty, but this doesn't mean that they have no problems. One person's problem may be less of a problem for someone else: a difficulty in one person's life may be a crisis in someone else's. You might like to think about this in terms of some of the characters in Hotspur Street. Often what matters is not just the problem itself but the circumstances in which the people concerned have to cope with it.

But do not imagine that it's your job to step in wherever *you* see problems. Knowing when to intervene in other people's lives, and when to stand back, is one of the most difficult and sensitive aspects of your job. Always remember that for most people their self-respect and their dignity are closely linked to their ability to look after themselves. Each of us likes to feel independent. Just as your independence is important to you, so the same will be true for all those people with whom you will come into contact as a care worker.

Classifying needs

Identifying and assessing people's needs is a key skill you need to develop. It's a complex process, partly because it usually involves a team of people, and partly because no two care situations are exactly alike.

It was sometimes found helpful to use a classification framework for grouping people in need. One such framework was introduced in Chapter 1 which was sometimes used by the social services to classify people whose needs were based on very similar sets of circumstances or similar medical conditions. Since you may see such categories referred to, or use them as part of a care report, it's as well to be familiar with them. The next task draws on your knowledge of the characters in the story, and demonstrates some of the complexities of identifying need.

▐▐▶ **TASK Classifying needs**
The six categories used in Chapter 1 to classify need were these:

- families with children;
- people with acute physical illness;
- people with physical disabilities;
- people with mental health difficulties;

	Families with children	Acute illness	Physical disabilities	Mental health difficulties	Older people	Special learning needs
Cath						
Bob						
Jenny						
Dave						
Zoë						
Nick						
Steve						
Tom						
Jane						

- older people;
- people with special learning-support needs.

The chart above lists nine of the people living in Hotspur Street whose lives you now know something about. Along the top are the six classifications of need. For each character, place an X in the category or categories you think relevant.■

✳ OBSERVATIONS
Completing this exercise may have caused you some problems – you probably found it difficult to fit some of the characters neatly into the categories provided. Dave, for example, can only be placed in the 'Families' category, yet this hardly identifies or throws light on his needs. Similarly, age may be one factor affecting Bob and Cath's well-being, but it's certainly not the significant explanation for their current needs. Likewise, Dave, Jenny and their children have immediate needs which aren't adequately reflected in their classification. They require emotional and social support, as well as access to the health services for the children's primary care and Jenny's postnatal care. As for Jane, her needs cannot be identified on this chart. She will require the support of her family to meet her physical and emotional needs while they are able to do so, but what happens when they are no longer able to care for her is not taken into account.

The effect of this classification is to produce a broad but often limited picture of people's individual needs, with the focus on the categories rather than the people. Such classifications are now recognised to be of limited use. They merely record the broad group or groups that each person fits into: they tell us little else

about the people or about their personal circumstances or the settings in which their needs arise. As we noted earlier, there are obvious dangers in trying to fit people into categories: caring is about individuals, not about groupings.■

IDENTIFYING NEEDS

It won't always be your personal responsibility to identify, assess and deal with people's needs – as we have seen, these responsibilities are usually shared with other people. Nevertheless, you will certainly be expected to contribute to these processes: to know what is involved, and to have the necessary skills and knowledge to play your part. Identifying and assessing need provide the basis for the decisions and action that follow, and good decisions are dependent on an accurate assessment of all the factors involved.

Making sense of the factors that underlie people's needs can be a complex business. The problems may be physical, mental, psychological, social, emotional or financial, and each of these may in turn be short- or long-term. Identifying the root causes of people's problems takes experience, skill and practice.

As we know, skills are developed through practice. The task that follows, which is in two parts, is designed to give you some practice in identifying and assessing needs.

▶ TASK Identifying needs (I)
The people living in Hotspur Street will inevitably have their share of needs – some obvious,

others less so. As you followed the action in the story you will have noted some of them.

Select *five* of the characters you have read about, and try to identify their needs. In each case, relate these needs to the categories that have been identified in the chart above, and add further categories if you wish. Think beyond the characters whose needs are visible, and therefore obvious, to those whose needs are less evident – people who may be coping, but who nonetheless may be at risk. It's the latter group of people who will put your professional skills to the real test.∎

✴ OBSERVATIONS

You may well have included Cath in your list: she is clearly a person at risk. Her needs may not all be obvious at first sight, yet she has real needs and these will be significant for her personally.

Cath and Bob are an active couple, enjoying a happy old age. We don't know whether Bob will survive the **stroke**, or **cerebrovascular accident** (**CVA**). Strokes usually affect older people, and can result in death or cause disability. A stroke is a disruption of the blood supply to the brain caused by thrombosis (blood clot), haemorrhage or embolus (a blood clot that moves from another part of the body), arterial disease or hypertension. The resulting signs and symptoms, which you may have learned about in GNVQ Unit 3, could include these:

- weakness or paralysis on the side of the body opposite to the affected side of the brain;
- difficulties with speech, if the left side of the brain is affected where the speech centre is situated in right-handed people;
- double or blurred vision;
- difficulty in swallowing;
- loss of emotional control.

There can be many physical and emotional complications for the person recovering from a stroke. A **rehabilitation** or **aftercare** programme, carefully planned by specialists from the health and care services, and the involvement of family and friends are essential. Because the patient may have no sensation in the affected side of the body, treatment should begin as soon as possible after the stroke. Even if the patient is unconscious, the initial stages of rehabilitation, through careful positioning and movement of the limbs, are of prime importance. **Recovery** after a stroke varies; health professionals will discuss possible **lifestyle changes** with the patient at the appropriate time.

Lisa acted quickly and efficiently during the emergency. She made sure Bob had an adequate **airway** and a **heartbeat**, and she carefully positioned his limbs so that he lay in the **recovery position**. When dealing with health emergencies, consider your own safety as well as the safety of the patient. As you work through the GNVQ, your tutors will emphasise this to you. Lisa, as you know, is a care assistant in a nursing home: although Cath was in a state of shock, she knew she must seek assistance from someone who could offer immediate help. Lisa did not enter into discussion with Cath until she had first assessed the situation for herself and taken the necessary emergency action. As Lisa showed, knowing how to act in an emergency can save lives.

Up to this point Lisa had been totally preoccupied with Bob's emergency situation. As a skilled care worker, however, she will have noted that Cath also will need help. Cath is in a state of shock and may, as a result, have physical needs that aren't obvious at first sight. Lisa will also know that a personal crisis of this sort will bring with it emotional problems for Cath. Finally, Cath's age may be significant in making her less able to cope with the personal crisis that has overtaken her. The effect of being alone may reduce her ability to manage emotionally.∎

⯈ TASK *Identifying needs (2)*

The second part of the task continues to focus on Cath. If she wasn't one of the characters you selected, simply take the observations above as your starting-point. The action in the story stops before we know what happens to Bob, but the chances are that the emergency care that he has received will ultimately lead to his return home. In the meantime Cath has been in the hands of her general practitioner (GP), who will have helped her to recover from the shock of Bob's CVA, if necessary offering medication to help stabilise her emotional condition.

Once Bob returns home, however, Cath's circumstances will change again, leading to an additional set of needs. The task this time is to try to identify in more detail what these needs might be, given Bob and Cath's new situation. Look for any new factors in Cath's life, assuming that Bob will be much more dependent upon her than he was previously. Remember, too, that at this stage he will be under medical supervision as part of a programme of recovery or rehabilitation.∎

✴ OBSERVATIONS

Your response ought to include one or more of the following:

- Cath will, in effect, become Bob's home carer. She will have to know how to make use of the available health and social care services.
- As home carer, Cath will have to meet Bob's immediate physical and emotional needs, and know something about how these might affect him.

PERSONAL PROFILE

There are 6.8 million carers of disabled and elderly relatives in Britain who need more recognition and support.

Cath Stewart (78) cares for her husband Bob (83), who had a stroke this year.

Hours 24 hours a day.

Support None from social services. Regular help with shopping, trips out and jobs around the house, from her children.

Income Bob's disability benefit: about £153 weekly. Her own retirement pension: £22.85 weekly. No carer's allowance: she is over retirement age.

Extra costs Hard to quantify. Heating about £150 a quarter; taxi fares £5 a week.

The job 'He is paralysed down one side. I do almost everything for him, washing him, helping dress him, cutting up his food, getting him in the bath. He's 6 foot and 11 stone, and I'm only 5 foot 2 inches. He can't even make a cup of tea. He can't be left alone in case of a fall.'

Pros 'I want to care; I wouldn't have it any other way. He'd do it for me if it was the other way round. I'm lucky I've still got him.'

Cons 'We are restricted. We don't have a car any more. We can't just go away for the weekend. I never go shopping. We were both looking forward to retirement, but it's changed all that.'

- Cath herself will continue to face a personal crisis as a result of Bob's illness, and will need emotional help and support.
- Cath will have to take on many of the everyday roles and responsibilities previously undertaken by Bob.∎

☞ POINTS TO REMEMBER

This exercise should have revealed several things, as well as giving you some practice at identifying and assessing people's needs. Check the points below, and make sure that you understand the significance of each. Go through them with your tutor if necessary, relating each to the kind of personal skills you should be developing through your study of the mandatory and core skill units, especially mandatory Units 1, 2 and 3.

A key skill here is that of **observation**: knowing how to observe people and situations, what to look for, and why people behave and react in the ways they do.

- *Some needs are evident* Identifying need is a comparatively straightforward skill when the need in question is clearly indicated by a visible change in the person's outward behaviour or condition. Thus, in the case of Tom a change in his personal circumstances appears to have triggered a significant change in his behaviour.
- *Others may be affected* A dramatic change in a person's circumstances may lead to changes in the lives of others close to them. Need can have a

'fallout' effect: it may bring changes to the lives of other people who are in every other respect coping perfectly adequately. Cath's situation illustrates these circumstances.

- *Not everyone will seek help* Many people don't wish to share their problems or concerns with others, yet may still be at risk. Being aware of, and identifying, such needs is more difficult; one person's reaction to a problem may not be the same as another's. Yasmin's determination to cope with her particular problems without support provides an example of this.
- *Personal factors* Significant clues about people's well-being are gained by considering their broader personal circumstances as well as assessing them as individuals. Bob's and Cath's needs are related to Bob's illness, to their age, to the absence of any immediate family around them, and to the changed roles and responsibilities they will be required to undertake.

If there is time, consider each of these points is turn. How does each point relate to the characters in the story who have not been mentioned so far? As you think about this, be mindful of how these points affect you in your role as a care worker.∎

ASSESSING NEEDS

As we have discovered, *identifying* need is not the same thing as *assessing* it. **Assessing** need is a matter of knowing enough about a situation to be able to take the necessary action to deal with it. This means understanding the precise nature of the needs involved, the factors behind them, and the issues involved in constructing a plan of action. Earlier we referred to this as making sense of situations: having the relevant information so that you can make appropriate decisions. Assessment is the critical link between identifying a need and producing a care plan to meet that need.

Care plans

There is no one way of constructing a **care plan** – each client's situation and needs will be unique. All care plans, however, are likely to include some or all of the following stages of development:

- identifying the client's condition and circumstances;
- assessing the client's needs and deciding on immediate action;
- setting longer-term goals and specific objectives;
- monitoring progress;
- evaluating the care plan.

These stages should remind you of the four GNVQ themes:

- planning;
- information seeking/handling;
- evaluation;
- quality of outcomes.

They should also remind you of the processes of action planning. Check that you can link each of the stages to one or more of the GNVQ themes and their related grading criteria. (If you need to look back to Chapter 3 for a review of the themes, do so.)

Assessment of need, leading to a care plan, may involve a formal procedure and be undertaken by specialists from the health and care services, or it may involve a referral procedure carried out by the care worker. This will depend on the nature of the person's needs. Thus Tom, you will remember, is awaiting an

Putting together a care plan

assessment of his needs by a social worker from the local authority social services department. This is a formal responsibility on the part of social services, and will eventually lead to the construction of a care plan involving a flexible programme of regular supervision, guidance and encouragement in order to meet Tom's immediate and longer-term needs. Where this kind of assessment is undertaken, remember that you will be part of the team responsible for putting the care plan into practice – you therefore need to understand how and why the decisions in the plan have been reached. This is crucial, as one of your duties will be to monitor the progress of the programme.

More often than not, though, people's needs are less critical than Tom's or Bob's, and formal care plans are unnecessary. In such cases the responsibility for identifying and assessing need and planning a course of action will be more informal and will rest with you. The process and skills involved, however, are much the same. Take Cath, for example: it would be your responsibility to assess her needs as part of the programme to rehabilitate Bob. The way we went about looking at Cath's needs would provide a starting-point for deciding what action is needed to help and support her in her new role as Bob's home carer.

Dependence and independence

The significant change in Cath's life is that she has suddenly become more **dependent** on others than she used to be. So have Bob and Tom, and so for that matter has Dave. People's needs are closely related to their ability to maintain sufficient **independence** so that they can live their lives as they would wish to. But this should not deceive us into thinking that we exist independently of each other – there is no such thing as true independence. Consider for a moment how many people you yourself have depended on since you got out of bed this morning. You will probably be quite surprised at the length of the list. The clothes you wear, the food you have eaten, the water, electricity, gas and other utilities you rely on in your home, the transport you used to get to school or college, the materials you are using in your studies, all reflect your dependence on the work and efforts of others, not least your family or others you live with.

Dependence upon others, then, is a perfectly normal part of our lives, and something we accept without question most of the time. Indeed, for the most part, it is something we enjoy and feel secure with. Each of the characters in the story is dependent on other people in their lives. Look back through the list of characters whose needs you classified at the beginning of this chapter, and note the ways in which these people depend on each other. What you find, of course, is that some people are more dependent than

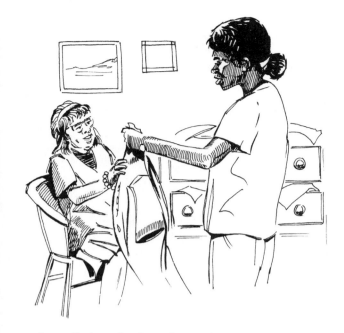

Jane will always be dependent on the support of others

others. As children, Zoë, Steve and Nick, for example, are very dependent on their parents, not just for their physical needs, but also for their emotional and social development. Lisa seems less dependent than most, whereas Tom has become very dependent on a whole variety of people. Jane is very dependent on her family, and it is clear that her independence will be limited for the rest of her life. However, there will be many decisions she *could* make for herself, such as choosing what to wear, what to eat and what to play with, and such points of independence should be encouraged.

Finding the right balance between dependence and independence is an important issue in everyone's life.

'Thank you for offering, but I'll do it myself'

Independence is a key quality in our well-being. It is something we value highly and try to hang onto at all costs: it contributes to our sense of self-respect and our sense of dignity. When independence is threatened or lost, many people find it particularly difficult to cope. If the loss happens unexpectedly, the difficulties are magnified.

Three of the characters in the story, Bob, Tom and Dave, have each suffered a serious loss of independence, though in very different ways. Their current needs are directly linked to the loss of personal independence. Providing support for such people, and for those dependent upon them, is often a matter of making good, as far as possible, the loss of their independence. Caring is always about helping people to look after themselves in a way that preserves their dignity and self-respect. In many cases this support is provided through specialist services, whether the assistance required be physical, emotional, social or financial; in others, as we've seen, support is provided by a professional care worker.

Dependence on others is a common and unavoidable feature of growing old, and most frequently affects this section of the population. We've noticed how Bob's, Cath's and Tom's circumstances are made more difficult by their old age, and age will certainly be a factor in any decisions made about their future welfare. There is an obvious danger, though, in linking old age and dependence too closely. Bob and Tom, for example, are well into their eighties, and at this age some deterioration in their health is to be expected. Jack, in contrast, is 62: though not yet formally categorised as old, Jack is leading a normal and active life and there is no reason to suppose that in three year's time his ability to look after himself will have altered radically.

Ageing and old age

Categorising people by age – or, for that matter, by any form of social, economic or cultural grouping – is not a helpful way of assessing their needs, or making judgements about them as individuals. You may have noticed that many people's perceptions of older people as a group can be very negative and dismissive. Older people are frequently portrayed as being an insignificant section of our society; stubborn, slow, forgetful, physically frail, and of little practical or economic importance to the rest of the population. Your experience in the last chapter of the negative images used to portray students should have taught you to beware of such perceptions. Many older people will feel just as you did, that negative preconceptions of this kind do not fit them personally.

Some facts and figures will show just how misleading such perceptions of older people are. By the year

Still going strong!

2000, one in five people in the UK will be over 60 years of age: this is not, therefore, an insignificant group in our society. Many older people are in full-time employment and contribute substantially to the nation's economy. Even more enjoy a full and active life, socially and culturally. Nor is health and fitness denied to older people: consider the age profile of the entrants to the London Marathon, a race run over 26 miles. Of the 25 000 entrants in 1994 nearly 5000 were over 50 years of age, 850 were over 60, and 102 were over 70. For many people, then, age is not a barrier to their involvement in the activities enjoyed by the rest of the population.

It's easy to portray groups in a negative light by taking some of the features of a minority of the group, such as the scruffiness of a few students, and presenting these as features of the whole group. When we do this we are said to be **discriminating** against the people who belong to such groups. This is an important term for you to understand and more will be said about it in the next chapter. It is covered in Element 4.2 of Mandatory Unit 4, and if you have already looked at it you will know that age is not the only basis for discrimination: race, disability, gender, wealth and class are also used as means to discriminate against particular groups of people. We shall return to this in the next chapter.

Caring involves promoting positive attitudes. Modern society is only just beginning to see the need to promote a positive image of ageing and to see old age as an important and fulfilling period in everyone's life. Remember that most people nowadays expect to live beyond 75 years of age: improved health care and better housing and nutrition have contributed to an increase in **life expectancy**. Ageing is not something that the care worker should see as a difficulty: everyone wants to be as independent as they can for as long as they can, and it's your job to help them achieve this.

Access to care and support for those older people who have experienced a loss of some independence is an important factor in promoting their well-being. (Mandatory Units 2, 3 and 4, and Elements 2.2, 3.2 and 4.3 examine this more closely.)

Continuing the focus on Bob and Cath in this section, we can now check two aspects of that support in relation to their immediate needs – rehabilitation or aftercare, and financial support.

Rehabilitation: Bob

In the story we are left not knowing whether Bob will survive the stroke – but let us assume that he *does* survive and is now about to be discharged from hospital to return home. Remind yourself of the possible after-effects of a stroke (mentioned earlier in the chapter), and be mindful that the effects can vary in severity.

Bob's rehabilitation will form the basis of the care plan put together by the care professionals to meet his needs. This plan will be based on a formal assessment of his needs, made before he leaves the security and relative safety of the hospital. It will focus on his ability to cope physically and emotionally in his own home, and will consider Cath's ability as his home carer, to cope with Bob's needs. There will be a lot for the professionals (including yourself) to consider before agreement can be reached about what is best for Bob and Cath. Let's just suppose that we are part of the team deciding on his care plan. What kinds of considerations and information will be needed in his assessment, and who will be responsible for what?

First, we shall need to know the extent of paralysis or weakness on the side of the body opposite to the affected side in the brain: this will be a factor in determining whether Bob will be able to cope in his own home. An **occupational therapist (OT)** will need to visit Cath in her home to find out whether Bob's rehabilitation can realistically take place there. There, and in the hospital, the OT will find the answers to a range of basic, practical questions such as:

- Where are the toilet and bathroom in relation to the bedroom? Are there any steps between the bedroom and the toilet or bathroom? Will Bob be able to turn on the taps, or will they need to be adapted?
- Will Bob be able to get from the bedroom to the sitting-room? Will he be able to sit in bed without special support, and will he need protection from the weight of the bedding? Can he sit in an easy chair without side supports?

- Will he be able to use drinking cups or will he need special spouts? Will he need cutlery with padded and enlarged handles?

Much will depend on whether any necessary aids can be provided through the social services or the health services. Cath's ability to assist Bob will also be a crucial factor in the assessment. If, for example, he requires a great deal of support in order to move around, then the fact that he is overweight would mean that Cath could not provide this support without help from care professionals – the home care workers, the physiotherapist, the occupational therapist, and possibly even the community nurse. Cath will also need to assist his recovery by helping him with the exercises devised by the physiotherapist.

Finally, Cath will need to be able to support Bob's emotional needs. Bob may be weepy and depressed. Strokes can affect emotional control. For Cath to see Bob upset over things he would normally have tackled will be distressing. The programme for Bob's rehabilitation will place a considerable burden of responsibility on Cath, and though the care professionals will be on hand to help and support her, they will need to be sure that Cath can herself cope before agreeing to Bob's return. Part of your job, as a care worker, would be to do all you could to see that Cath received the support, love and affection of her family, friends and neighbours – and, of course, of yourself.

Financial support: Bob

Once Bob returns home he will face significant changes in his lifestyle. There are likely to be increases in expenditure, owing to additional heating, laundry, and possibly food costs. Most elderly people are excellent at living on a fixed budget – they have no choice. In Bob and Cath's case, their own budget may be supplemented by further financial assistance to which they are entitled because of their particular situation.

You need to know about such supplementary assistance, as well as knowing about the normal levels of financial support to which all senior citizens are entitled as of right. Obtaining this information for yourself provides a useful opportunity for a 'finding out' task.

IIII➡ TASK Financial support

This task is split into two parts: the first deals with the entitlements of all elderly people in terms of financial support from the State; the second relates specifically to Bob and Cath. Additional financial entitlements are directly linked to particular needs, so the questions asked in this part of the task are based

on what you already know about Bob's physical condition at the time of his discharge from hospital. No answers are given, so check your findings with your tutor, or through relevant literature provided by the Department of Social Security. Knowing where and how to obtain such information is an important aspect of your training; having done so will help you provide evidence of your ability to meet the GNVQ grading criteria.

1 General entitlement

Find out the answers to the following questions:

- What is the official retirement age from employment for men and women, after which they are entitled to a State pension?
- How much money would Cath and Bob receive each week in pension allowance?
- How much would Bob or Cath receive if the other should die?

2 Additional financial entitlements

In the light of what you know about Bob and Cath's circumstances, indicate which of the supplementary allowances Bob and/or Cath would be entitled to.

- Free prescriptions?
- Free eye tests?
- Free public transport?
- Heating allowance?
- Free home care?
- Sickness benefit?
- Attendance allowance?∎

Identifying needs: Tom

Like Bob and Cath, Tom belongs to the 'older people' category. But there the similarities end. Tom's main problem lies with his mental health. In order to make a sensible assessment of Tom's needs it is necessary to go back into an earlier period in his life. For him, the significant change or **life event** was the death of his daughter, Mildred. Since then Tom has become disorientated and confused. He was probably used to an organised life with a routine to it that gave him reassurance as well as a structure in each day. Because children usually outlive their parents, when they don't, the natural order in the human cycle is upset. This may help to explain Tom's recent behaviour.

Tom is approaching the final stages of his life. Like most elderly people, he has probably come to terms with the inevitability of his own death. But still he may not have accepted Mildred's death, having thought that she would outlive him. We don't know whether he understands what has happened, or whether he is aware of the consequences of not being able to cope in his own home. He has neighbours who are helping as much as they can, but a crisis appears to be developing.

Grief and shock

Tom's grief is a natural emotion following such a significant life event. Feelings of shock, disbelief, anger, depression, and eventually acceptance after the death of a loved one are all perfectly normal. How well the bereaved person copes with the emotions associated with death often depends on the circumstances in which the person died.

People frequently respond to bereavement by trying to make sense of what has happened. They may want to explore the reasons for the death and ask why or how it happened, to try to restore some sort of order so that they understand the events leading up to the death. Seemingly, Tom has not been able to go through the stages of grieving because he has become **disorientated**, or very confused. This has resulted in his inability to cope with day-to-day living needs.

Assessing needs: Tom

Tom is no longer in a position to look after himself. Despite the efforts of his neighbours and friends in Hotspur Street, his case must now be referred to the health and care services for specialist help. This will involve a full and formal assessment of Tom's situation, conducted in this instance by a social worker from social services. This will lead to the development of a care plan designed to meet Tom's physical, mental and emotional needs. The plan will aim to restore Tom to a life that preserves as much personal independence for him as is possible – most people who rely on help because they are housebound or mentally or physically disabled don't want to be cared for in an institution. Providing for Tom's needs in his own home will require a programme of rehabilitation.

Rehabilitation: Tom

As we saw with Bob's rehabilitation, the idea is to provide people with enough support to regain the lost structure and purpose in their lives. This will only be achieved with the help, guidance and supervision of a range of professionals within the health and care services, including a care worker. Others in the team might include:

- a home help;
- a community nurse;
- an occupational therapist;
- a social worker;
- a general practitioner (GP);

- a community psychiatric nurse;
- a care attendant or home care assistant;
- meals on wheels;
- a visiting service.

Tom's situation would entitle him to support from several of these services. We'll be dealing with the health and care services more fully in Chapter 7, but it would be useful at this stage for you to know something about the services available, what they offer and who is involved. Notice that the care worker is listed as part of the team: knowing how you fit into the service is very important.

Rehabilitation

▐▶ TASK Identifying home support needs

This task involves looking at the home support care that Tom may need. Let's begin at a very practical level. Go back to the story and remind yourself of the extent to which Tom is able to look after himself, and consider what sorts of everyday things he might need help with. The story won't offer you answers, but it will give you enough idea of Tom's condition to make a reasonable guess at his needs.

Having done that, look at the chart on page 57 and tick the care tasks with which you think Tom needs help. At the same time, try to identify which service or person is responsible for providing the support you have indicated. If you've started work on Elements 3.1 and 3.3 in Unit 3, 'Health and Social Care Services', you may already know the answers; if not, ask your tutors or your workplace supervisor for advice. You are more likely to find the answers from people who are familiar with the job than from books.▐

Care	Tom's needs	Professional worker/service
Washing/bathing		
Toileting		
Dressing		
Cooking		
Cleaning		
Shopping		
Talking		
Activities (e.g. hobbies, going out)		
Aids to living (e.g. bath grips, handrails)		

Mental health needs: Tom

As well as responding to Tom's everyday practical needs, his rehabilitation programme will need to address his mental health problems. The story doesn't tell us a great deal about him but we do know that he is vulnerable and possibly in danger of accidentally harming himself. We know that Tom is confused, and it has been suggested already that his unusual behaviour is probably a consequence of Mildred's death. We can't actually know how he is really feeling; nonetheless, it's possible with imagination to get some idea of his situation.

Try to imagine waking up one morning to find that everything in your bedroom is unfamiliar. You look around: there is nothing that you recognise. You turn on the radio to find the presenter speaking in a language you don't understand. You look out of the window where there are no familiar landmarks. You look at your watch, but you can't see any numbers on the face. You try to open the bedroom door, to get out, but it is firmly locked . . . . *Panic!* You feel the palms of your hands go sticky; you breathe more quickly, and your heart rate increases. You cannot understand what is going on – you feel very scared. You close your eyes for a moment – when you open them, your bedroom is back to normal and the familiar, everyday things have returned. Was it all a dream?

There is no simple explanation as to why people imagine that events are taking place when it is clear

to others around them that they are not. Tom's confusion is not caused by drugs, though he is being prescribed sleeping tablets to try to keep him calm. His confusion has resulted in him seeing things and people that do not exist. This can happen as people grow old and if their physical and mental well-being deteriorate because of unfamiliar circumstances or because of significant and unexpected changes in their lives. Mildred's death seems to have been the trigger for Tom's decline. It is very important to try to maintain Tom's independence by providing professional care in his own home. If he were admitted, even for a short time, into an institution of any sort, the change in environment could result in him becoming even more confused.

One way of supporting Tom might be to try to aid his **reorientation**, helping him to get in touch with what is going on in the real world around him. This practice is often referred to as **reminiscence therapy** or **reality orientation therapy**. It takes time. The process involves using memories from a person's recent and distant past and, over a period of weeks, getting them to share these with others. Gradually the person begins to remember the importance of various events and people in his or her life. In Tom's case, the memory of Mildred and her place in his life will play a major part in his therapy.

If you want to find out more about such therapy, ask your tutor, or those helping and supporting you in the workplace.

POINTS TO REMEMBER

This chapter has focused mainly on the needs of the older section of the population. Nevertheless, it should have helped to develop your knowledge and understanding of people in general, whatever their age. Though older people frequently have particular needs, they are part of the same society as the rest of us and contribute to the shaping of its attitudes and values, just as we all do. They are not a different or a separate group of people. Like all of us they are individuals who may need special help at certain moments in their lives: at other times they have the right to enjoy the same entitlements and opportunities as everyone else.

Besides these general considerations, there are a number of specific points to bear in mind when caring for older people. Many of these points give rise to general principles relating to everyone in need of care, as the next chapter will show.

1 Ageing is a process that happens to each of us but not to everyone at the same rate nor in exactly the same way.
2 Older people are vulnerable to sudden and unexpected changes to their circumstances.

Because of their age, many such changes are difficult to cope with without support.

3 Growing old does not mean becoming a burden on the rest of the population. Many older people enjoy very independent and active lives and contribute significantly to the nation's economy.

4 Older people, like everyone else, value their independence highly. Independence contributes to their sense of self-respect and dignity.

5 Perceptions of older people as stubborn, forgetful and incapable are not an accurate view of most older people. This picture is a negative image which fosters discrimination against old people in general.

6 Because increased dependence on others sooner or later is an inevitable part of growing old, support and help for this age group are provided as a matter of entitlement to meet many of their needs.

IIII➡ TASK: Time for reflection
Before going on to the next chapter, think about how each of these points, extended as general principles, might apply to any group of people or individual.

Finally, cast your mind back to Jane in the story. She belongs to a group of people identified as having physical or psychiatric/mental health disabilities or both. In the light of what you know about Jane so far, and from the work you may by now have covered in mandatory Units 2 and 3, consider each of the points made above in relation to someone with a disability. (This will provide the groundwork for a more detailed task in the next chapter.)

Finally, one last thought on people with disabilities. Look at the photograph below of one of the competitors in the 1995 London Marathon. What does it tell you about people with disabilities?▪

KEY WORDS AND TECHNICAL TERMS

Arterial disease Any disease affecting the arteries, such as the narrowing caused by atheroma formation (fatty deposits). Angina pectoris is one example of a condition caused by arterial disease.

Bereavement The condition resulting from the loss of something or someone special to you. The term is most commonly applied to the loss, through death, of a close family member or friend.

Care plan A detailed plan of action designed to meet someone's care needs. It is put together by a team of professionals in the light of an assessment of the person's needs, and has clearly defined goals and expected outcomes. A care plan also identifies how its application will be monitored and evaluated.

Classification The arrangement of things into groups on the basis that they have certain features in common. People, too, can be classified: you, for example, can be classified for some purposes as 'a student'.

Community nurse A health professional who provides nursing care for those who need it in their own homes. (Community nurses used to be called district nurses.)

Community psychiatric nurse A health professional who provides care, supervision and support for those with mental health problems who are living in their own homes, or in hostels, or in a community setting.

Congenital Describes a condition that has existed from birth.

Discrimination The process of making distinctions between groups of things or people, and reaching judgements about them based on the preconceptions you hold of them. Discrimination is therefore based on prejudice.

Disorientation A state of confusion in which a person loses his or her sense of time, location, and personal awareness.

Embolism The blockage of an artery by any solid material, such as a blood clot or an air bubble, which has moved from the place where it formed.

General practitioner A family doctor who provides primary health services.

Genetic inheritance The characteristics that we inherit from our parents through the transmission of their genes.

Health services The services provided by the National Health Service (NHS). These are discussed in Chapter 7.

Independence The state in which a person can look after himself or herself and not to need to rely on other people for the basic necessities in life. In this sense young children are not independent, nor are some elderly people or people with disabilities if they cannot cope without help. Independent people are largely in control of their own lives and decisions.

Life event An event of exceptional significance in a person's life, such as a death in the family, or a divorce.

Life expectancy The number of years we can expect to live, based on national averages.

Medication Treatment with medicine or prescribed drugs.

Nutrition The intake of nourishment to the body, usually as food and drinks. Nutrients feed the body so that it can function properly.

Occupational therapist A health professional who provides treatment to help the recovery of people suffering from physical and mental illness. Occupational therapy is a particular form of care which helps people to see how they can most easily cope with the everyday activities of life.

Paralysis A loss of feeling or movement in some affected part of the body, caused by damage to the nervous system.

Physiotherapist A health professional who provides physical activities and exercises to help people recover after injury, illness or surgery.

Postnatal care Care provided by various members of the health services (such as a midwife and a health visitor) for mothers, for six weeks after the birth of their children.

Primary care The services provided by the health professionals who act as the first line of call when help is needed – family doctors, dentists, community nurses, and the like (see Chapter 7).

Psychological Relating to the mind. Psychology is the study of the human mind and the way it functions.

Rehabilitation A programme specially put together by health and care professionals to aid someone's recovery from illness. Bob's recovery, for example, will be dependent on the rehabilitation programme designed for him.

Reminiscence therapy A form of care used to help people who are disorientated to recover their sense of time, space and personal awareness. It uses past events in their lives to help them get back in touch with the real world.

Reorientation The process of recovering one's bearings – the process of returning from a confused state of mind to one which experiences a realistic sense of time, space and personal awareness.

6 • Caring in action

This chapter looks at some ways in which people for whom you may be caring may be affected by factors outside their immediate situations. In this chapter you will:

- consider how people's well-being is affected by the influences of the communities and societies in which they live;
- examine, through the Hotspur Street story, particular influences of the family upon people's attitudes and values;
- examine, through the example of Dave and his family in the story, the impact of some of the economic factors that affect people's lives;
- explore further the material covered in the GNVQ mandatory Units 2 and 4, through the action presented in the story;
- reconsider the key skills and abilities required to meet the demands and responsibilities of being a care worker.

As you've worked through the book, you may have noticed how the focus has gradually shifted from looking at you as a person to looking at other people or groups in society, while all the time stressing that each of us, in our own way, is only one part of a much larger picture. This chapter has two purposes. First, it continues to broaden this focus, and to bring into range (do you remember this term?) other people in the Hotspur Street story whose lives are significantly affected by different factors. Their experiences and needs will illustrate principles governing a great many people's lives, and help you to extend your thinking about some of the key issues introduced in the last two chapters. (This work will link directly into the work covered in the GNVQ mandatory Units 2 and 4.)

The second purpose of this chapter is to review the key skills and understandings required of you as a future care worker. Because the approach used in this book has been to look at caring through action, these abilities have been identified as the need has arisen, rather than treated as separate areas for study or training. They are summarised in an extended 'Points to remember' section at the end of the chapter.

SOCIETY, COMMUNITY AND FAMILY

At some point in the book, each of these three groupings – *society, community* and *family* – has been used with reference to people, or groups of people, in the story. We have also thought a lot about *individuals*, and how they fit into, and influence, these broader groupings. There is a parallel in the relationship between the elements and the units here with your GNVQ programme: each element and unit, you will recall, has its own identity and purpose, but each also has links with others; together they combine to form a unified programme of education and training.

In the same way, societies, communities and families aren't separate groups of different people: they overlap. Each of us belongs to a family, a community, and a society.

Let's use what we know about Zoë from the story to show how this works. Zoë is an individual belonging to a family of five. She has two parents and two brothers; she may have other family or relations, but the story doesn't tell us this. We know that she and her family belong to a community located around Hotspur Street. The community consists of neighbours, friends, and probably people who meet at work or in shops, and so on. Finally, the community around Hotspur Street is situated within a town, and is therefore surrounded by other local communities, each made up of further families and individuals within them. Together with all the people living elsewhere in Britain, the inhabitants of Hotspur Street make up British society.

But even this model makes things seem simpler than they really are. It may suggest, for example, that each grouping consists of people who are all very much alike. Yet this is not the case. As members of the British society, for example, we may all be subjects of the same monarch and subject to the same Parliament at Westminster, but beyond that there is little else that we *all* share fully in common. People in Scotland, for instance, have their own legal system and their own education system; and their currency still includes pound notes. Likewise, English is not the only language spoken in Britain: for a lot of people,

English is their second language, and for some it is a language that they cannot speak at all. Similarly, the dominant culture in Britain is European, but other cultures are important here, too.

On closer inspection, then, it's a bit like a patchwork quilt, with lots of different pieces of different sizes and shapes all fitting together to make something larger. Some patches are the same, some similar, others very different. Some groups, like the family, are small; others, such as communities, are much larger; and societies are larger still. Families differ from each other, as do communities and societies. People and situations are never exactly alike, and groupings of people are just as complex as the individuals who belong to them.

Social units

One approach is to regard groupings such as families, communities and societies as **social units** which help people to organise and live their lives. A significant feature of each group is the **code of rules** which identifies what's expected of those who belong to the group. In societies these may be formalised as laws; in schools and colleges they may be regulations, and in families merely expectations. Rules give people a feeling of relative security. The common code also helps them to support each other when the need arises, because groups develop a sense of belonging, or **group identity**, which makes those in them feel a responsibility towards each other, a wish to give to the group as well as take from it.

Groups have other purposes, too. Many exist in order to provide opportunities for people to share similar interests – such groups are frequently formed in order to pursue sporting or other leisure and cultural activities. Spend a few moments thinking about the groups *you* belong to, and why. In various ways they will be helping you to organise and enjoy your life, as well as providing frameworks within which you in turn are required to meet certain expectations and standards in your life.

The other striking feature about groups, as well as the people in them, is their **diversity**. Diversity means variety, or lots of differences, which is why it is so often used when describing people and the ways that they organise their lives. Like the pieces in the patchwork quilt, people are not just different, they are different in a variety of ways.

Recognising and accepting this principle is a key aspect of working with people. So is the conclusion that diversity does not mean that one particular group of people is better or worse than another; merely that they are different. Such understandings underpin the work you will cover in Unit 4, Element 2, on discrimination, and are also important in relation to what follows in this chapter.

Community

The story of Hotspur Street is set within a community on the outskirts of a large town. The people we meet there seem to be a diverse group of people illustrating the variety of differences highlighted above. This kind of community may be familiar to you, or alternatively, it may be remote from your own experience. If you have time, compare your experience from the communities that you yourself have lived in with the experiences of other members of your group.

What features did they have in common? If Hotspur Street is anything to go by, one similarity will be the way that people help and support each other. Hotspur Street is apparently a particularly strong and involved community, perhaps because it's a relatively small place. A sense of belonging is easier to achieve in smaller places where it's possible for most people to know each other – though this can also have its drawbacks! Even so, the feeling one gets from TV programmes such as *Coronation Street* and *EastEnders*, which are based on communities situated in large cities, is that the people who live in such communities also see themselves as belonging to one large family. In this sense they don't seem very different from the people in Hotspur Street.

So, communities are assumed to possess strong personal links between the people living in them, and for this reason they have provided a focus for local health and social care provision. As you will know from your GNVQ course, the NHS and Community Care Act 1990 has sought to strengthen these links and relationships in a number of ways. One has been to give added responsibility to workers providing care in people's own homes. The effect has been to make many of those in need of care, and many of those providing care, much more dependent on the services in the local community and on the people living there.

By far the most important link in this chain is the family. Indeed, some have argued that the idea of 'the caring community' is greatly exaggerated in modern Britain: they say that it is the family that bears, and will continue to bear, the real burden and responsibility for providing care in the community.

The family

The family provides the basic social unit from which communities and societies are constructed. The majority of people are members of families, though – as with most things to do with people – the term 'family' will mean different things to different people. When you hear someone refer to 'my family', you cannot be sure whether they mean the people they live with and to whom they are related, or to their more distant relatives, or to some other group unique to them.

In our society we like to believe that the family is a happy and settled group of people who are biologically related and who live together in harmony. In many circumstances such a family would comprise the father, who is also the wage earner, and the mother, who stays at home to cook, to clean and to provide comfort to dependent children, and the children themselves. This is not necessarily how it really is.

Many groups of people live together harmoniously but do not match this traditional family model. Examples include a large household of people of mixed sex and age, or two women with dependent children sharing the same home and their responsibilities: these may be different from the traditional family model, but such groupings can be just as effective and acceptable. Other groups of people might define themselves as 'a family', even though they aren't biologically related. For example, a man and woman with two adopted children will feel like a family, behave like a family, and be seen by others as a family.

Family classification

Not surprisingly, efforts have been made to find ways of defining the different types of family arrangements that exist. The following is a typical example:

- *Nuclear family* Parents and children geographically separated from other family members.

- *Extended family* Children, parents and grandparents sharing the same home.

- *Single-parent family* Only one parent, with a child or children.

Extended family

Nuclear family: separated geographically

Single-parent family

Reconstituted family

- *Reconstituted family* A couple, one or both of whom have children from an earlier partnership, living with their children – who may share both parents, only one parent, or neither parent.

⫸ TASK Classifying families

Using these definitions, classify the families represented within the story.∎

Family member(s)	Family classification
Cath and Bob	
Jenny, Dave and children	
Tom	
Jane	
Yasmin, Abdul and children	
Lisa	

✸ OBSERVATIONS

As we've found previously, classifying people is not a straightforward process. Sometimes we don't know enough about the people concerned; at other times they won't fit into the categories provided. Dave, Jenny and their family fit simply the normal pattern in our society, that of the nuclear family.

Tom, on the other hand, lives alone and has no family that we know of – he can't, therefore, be classified.

Why do we need to classify families? One reason is to consider how best to allocate welfare benefits and assistance such as income support and family credit. Other purposes may be less obviously helpful. Families are sometimes referred to as belonging to a particular social class – as being 'middle class' or 'working class' – categories often arrived at on the basis of people's occupations. This is called **social classification**, and is widely used by Government to describe the composition of society in Britain. The table below is the one used by the Registrar General to categorise people into social classes according to their occupations.∎

Social classification	
Social class	*Types of occupation*
Class I: Professional	Doctors, judges, lawyers, architects, scientists
Class II: Managerial and technical	Teachers, nurses, managers, occupational therapists
Class III: Skilled (non-manual)	Photographers, footballers, driving instructors, clerks
Class III: Skilled (manual)	Bricklayers, plasterers, carpenters, plumbers
Class IV: Partly skilled	Traffic wardens, farm workers, bus conductors
Class V: Unskilled	Messengers, labourers, cleaners

Source: Registrar General, 'Social Class based on Occupations', taken from *Standard Occupational Classification (SOC)*, Vol. 3 (1991)

Social classification

All the people in the first three of the social classes in the table are employed in non-manual occupations, and are generally regarded as belonging to 'the middle class'. Those in the last three categories are manual workers and tend to be seen as being in 'the working class'.

Whatever their intended purpose, one effect of such classifications is to link social class with contrasting beliefs, behaviours and attitudes. People said to belong to the middle class are regarded as having different attitudes and values to those belonging to the working class. The following examples are fairly typical. Bingo is a game associated with the working class, whereas bridge is associated with the middle class. Going to the theatre is something the middle class do; the working class prefer the cinema. The two classes are presumed to be divided by different political preferences, different attitudes towards education, and so on. Doubtless you can think of lots of other ways in which the behaviours and values of the two classes are seen as being different. Spend a few minutes drawing up a list of some of the differences that are thought to exist.

What you have done is to create a general picture of each of the social classes, which can then be used to define the character and membership of that class. The picture shows how the members of that class or group are viewed, and even how they are expected to behave. Such a description refers to the **norm**: the behaviour and values of the *majority* of people in any group. It's what makes them a definable group, and different from other groups.

We have already been alerted to the dangers of this kind of approach. Not every individual in a group exactly matches the norm for that group; indeed, it's likely that no single member in any group reflects *all* of its norms. Check the list of behaviours and values that you identified for the two social classes. Do you personally fit all of the norms for either of the groups? It's the same old issue, of course: as individuals we are all different.

A further shortcoming is that norms provide the basis for the ways that people are expected to behave. Because the norm is the standard set by the majority of the people in a group, it's easy for that standard to become the basis for what is then regarded as *acceptable* behaviour within the group as a whole. The norm provides a means of making judgements about the behaviour of every person within the group, and awarding differences of status according to whether or not the individual adopts the group norms. Often people who behave differently, or who have different values or attitudes from the majority in the group, are represented as being of less worth.

This practice also occurs across social groups. The middle class, through their occupations and positions within the economy, have a higher status than the working class. For this reason, their beliefs and attitudes are often regarded as being more acceptable than those of the working class. Again this is an unhelpful outcome of using classification systems to categorise people. The classification provides grounds for discrimination against particular individuals and groups of people who, for whatever reason, do not reflect the group norms.

Element 2.3 in Unit 2 covers the topic of group roles and classification systems in greater detail. What is important is that you understand not only how social classification systems work, but also their effects on the ways that individuals can exist, and the ways in which individuals and groups are perceived by others, within society. You need to be able to apply your knowledge of social systems to your professional practice. As has just been said, there is a link between categorising people and discrimination: when you come to Element 4.2 in Unit 4, think about how the work covered in Element 2.3 helps to explain discrimination against particular individuals and groups within society. Reflect, too, upon how this work relates to the examples of discrimination identified in Chapter 5. (This is a good illustration of what is meant by an integrated approach to learning.)

Your knowledge and learning through the GNVQ units will link into your performance and your responsibilities as a care worker. Take what you now know about families. As we've seen, they can take many forms; nevertheless, there *is* a traditional family model within our society, the nuclear family. This serves as the norm, and is the standard against which other family models are often judged. Those departing from this model are frequently regarded as less acceptable, as can be seen in the attitudes of some people towards one-parent families, or towards families in which the parents are unmarried. Such attitudes may be quite hostile, to the extent that the families involved really do feel themselves to be the targets of discrimination.

It's important to realise that there are good arguments to be made about both the strengths and the weaknesses of each model of the family. It isn't for you in your professional role to decide that one is more acceptable than another. Your job is to *accept* the principle of diversity and to understand that the differences you encounter in practice often have as much to do with the changing economic and social circumstances around us as with the personal choice of those involved.

Never jump to hasty conclusions about other people's lives just because they differ from your own, or from the majority of other people's. It's always a mistake to make judgements about people's values and lifestyles in this way. Can you think of any **value judgements** that some people might make about any of the people living in Hotspur Street?

THE INFLUENCE OF THE FAMILY

Family roles

An important feature of families are the **roles** played within them by family members. Not so long ago these roles were more or less agreed. The norm was the traditional family model described earlier, but this model is no longer realistic in today's Britain, as Dave and Jenny's situation illustrates. Each family does what seems best for them as a unit.

For instance, women in paid employment are now an increasingly important part of the economy, and many women combine family life with a job. It

'Bye, have a good day at work'

- Do some members have more roles than others? Who? Why?
- Are some roles seen to be more important than others? Which ones? Who takes on these roles? Why?
- Do members of your family behave differently in their roles at home from the way they behave in their roles outside the home? In what ways? Why?
- Do you behave differently in your role as student from the way you behave at home? In what ways? Why?
- Do people in your family exchange roles? What sort of roles do they exchange, and why?
- Do any members of your family take on roles in order not just to get the jobs done but also to show other members how to behave and what's expected of them? How?

You should by now realise that roles play an important part in your family's well-being, as well as in getting the jobs done! Roles reflect status: because of this they often influence the way we see and treat others, as well as the way we see ourselves. Roles are very much part of our self-identity. The roles we're willing to take on are not always a matter of having the time to carry them out: just as often what matters is whether we feel that they fit our image of ourselves.

You may have realised, too, that roles give others patterns to copy and learn from. Typically, parents 'set an example' to their children. This we call **role modelling**. Psychologists have shown that role modelling has a very powerful influence on children's learning and development.

Primary socialisation

For most children it's the family that provides their first experience of relating to other people. The character and quality of family relationships will therefore play an important part in the way their attitudes and personalities are formed and developed.

It's remarkably difficult to break away from the norms and behaviours that we believe are expected of us, and early parental influences are of critical importance. Steve and Nick, for instance, may be given traditional boys' toys, and Zoë may be exposed to girls' toys. Only in recent years have childhood experiences and their effect on the roles and attitudes in adulthood been fully explored. Influences on children can affect future behaviours and expectations dramatically. Steve and Nick may not experience playing with traditional toys for girls, such as dolls, prams and house-play toys, until their sister is older: by that time it may be too late for them to play with these in an uninhibited way. Their own gender roles and expectations may already be fixed.

usually works out, however, that it is the woman who takes a career break in order to stay at home with the baby, while the man continues to go out to work. Occasionally a woman will choose to return to full-time employment after the birth of a child, and the male partner may stay at home and be the main carer.

Since many of the roles within the family can be undertaken by more than one member, it's possible for families to have some choice about what suits their interests best. On Tuesdays, for example, the eldest child may cook dinner, while the second eldest walks the dog, the father does the ironing, and the mother works late. This is a long way from the traditional, rather sentimental, picture of the ideal mother who looks after the home while the father goes out to paid employment and the children go off to school.

TASK Identifying family roles
Identify the roles played by members of *your* family. At the same time, begin to think about what lies behind these roles. The following questions will help to focus your thinking.

This is known as **primary socialisation**. In effect, Nick and Steve will already have in their minds models of the roles that they will expect to play later in their lives. Being given toys that are 'for boys' rather than 'for girls' provides them with a gender model of what it means to be a man, as opposed to a woman, and what it means to be a father, as opposed to a mother. Socialisation may also give them the idea that one role is more important than another, for example that the traditional 'male' role of breadwinner has higher status than the 'female' role of nurturer, because it is associated with providing the money the family needs in order to live.

This is only one example among hundreds of ways in which our ideas and attitudes are formed and developed, perhaps unintentionally, through our family upbringing. More often than not, these family attitudes reflect the norms and **values** of the community in which we live, or of society in general. These values are then used to define the **culture** of that group. A whole range of expectations and assumptions unite members of that culture: the way they dress, what they see as right and wrong, their attitude to work, the way they speak, the food they eat, their attitude towards the roles of men and women, their attitude towards marriage, their religious beliefs, and even their attitudes towards children.

By the age of 3 most children, through their experiences within the family, are well on the way to being socialised into society's assumptions and cultural norms. The process is continued at school. In recent years strenuous efforts have been made in schools to ensure that the learning environment for children, especially very young children, is based on a principle of **equal opportunity** for all. Schools try to avoid the suggestions that certain people should be valued more highly than others, that certain occupations are better suited to men than to women or vice versa, that one culture is superior to another, that the views of one group of people are more important than the views of others, and so on.

Bearing all of this in mind, let's go back to the action in the story, and in particular to Dave, Jenny and their family.

Identity and self-esteem

The crisis in Dave's life is mainly bound up with family roles, and the assumptions that lie behind these. He's not suffering from any physical illness. In one sense, identifying his problem is quite straightforward: he's lost his job, a fairly common occurrence these days. Sadly he's been unable to find another one, which again is not uncommon for many people of Dave's age. What we see now is a marked change in his behaviour towards Jenny and his

children. He shows little interest in any of them or, indeed, in himself. Without adequate support, Jenny in turn is beginning to feel the stress of trying to cope single-handed with the children, while at the same time encouraging and standing by her husband.

So, what's Dave's real problem? It isn't so much the fact that he is unemployed as that he feels he is failing in his role as a father. Seen through his eyes, it is his responsibility, as the father in the family, to provide for the other members. Though a somewhat outdated view of the male role in the modern family, it remains a very powerful one. For Dave, as for many men, the role provides the mirror in which he perceives himself. What he sees now is a person failing to meet the expectations he thinks others have of him, failing to live up to the values associated with fatherhood.

Dave's situation shows vividly how emotional security comes about through the way we feel about ourselves, and the way we think others feel about us. The term used to describe this feeling is **self-esteem**. (By now you should know quite a lot about this from the work you have covered in mandatory Unit 4, Element 4.3.) The more emotional security we have, the stronger our self-esteem or self-worth becomes. We place a value upon ourselves. This feeling of 'self', of our individuality, gives us a sense of purpose in what we do.

Being made redundant has altered Dave's sense of identity and as a result has affected his emotional well-being. You will know from your work in Elements 4.2 and 4.3 that tackling such problems as a care worker takes a lot of skill and patience. Most important of all, remember that what would matter would be respecting *Dave's* feelings and seeing things through *his* eyes, not your own. Listening would be a key skill.

LABELLING, STEREOTYPING AND DISCRIMINATION

You may already have noted that there is a link between Dave's problems and one possible effect of identifying people as 'different' because they cannot – or choose not to – follow the normal pattern of behaviour. Such people are often made to feel failures in the eyes of others. Dave's inability to fulfil what he sees as his family responsibilities is one reason why he may feel rejected. Being unemployed is becoming more common these days, but still this may make him conscious of having failed to meet the 'normal' expectations for people of his age.

Referring to people by categories that they fall into, rather than seeing them as individuals, is known as **labelling**. Dave, for example, could be labelled as 'unemployed'. This might be harmless enough were it not for the fact that being unemployed frequently attracts negative reactions, particularly from those who have jobs. You may have heard it said, for example, that people who are unemployed are lazy, that they don't like work and prefer to live off the State. Making judgements and assumptions about people on the basis of the behaviour and attitudes of a small minority of them is called **stereotyping.** (Recall the earlier discussion about descriptions of the 'typical' student, which are an excellent example of stereotyping.) Such perceptions are frequently based on **prejudice** and bias, and usually arise from ignorance of the real situation. Make sure that you fully understand each of the key terms used above. They are all factors in the process of **discrimination**. So far, we have concentrated mainly on discrimination against groups of people – the elderly, for example. We might just as easily have chosen to identify people with disabilities, black people, or women. Spend some time, ideally with your tutors, identifying ways in which members of *these* groups might feel discriminated against. Try to do this by thinking of them as groups, and not as particular individuals. You might feel, for example, that in general women are discriminated against, making it harder for them to get certain jobs, or to get promotion. Is there equality of opportunity and treatment for all members of these groups?

Discrimination can take many forms, some obvious and direct, others more subtle and hidden. Dave is suffering because he feels a form of discrimination that is an invisible part of our culture: the way we're made to feel even without anyone directly telling us. Language can have this effect on the lives and confidence of people. Take the position of women, for instance. Consider how often the word 'man' is used to define occupations (postman, milkman, taxman) as well as positions of status (chairman), even when it is women who are doing these jobs. Why are men who cook called 'chefs', but women who cook called 'cooks'? Language carries hidden messages which are important factors in identifying the place and relative status of certain groups and individuals in society.

A further form of discrimination affects the individual much more directly: **personal abuse** and **victimisation**. Examples are name-calling, bullying, excluding people from activities, and, worst of all, physical violence against the person concerned. The increase in these types of discrimination, particularly against minority groups, is a frightening trend in today's society.

Dealing with discrimination

Recognising and understanding the nature of discrimination is one thing: dealing with it is another. There is no easy answer: every situation in which it occurs will be different, and each has to be dealt with individually. On some occasions it is necessary or helpful to confront an incident of discrimination as it arises, but this needs care: it's easy to make things worse instead of better. Ultimately, discrimination ceases when people understand what they are doing and feel responsible for their own actions, but this is hard to achieve. Getting people to understand something has a better chance of success if you yourself are offering a positive role model. Never expect more from others than you expect from yourself.

FAMILY LIFE AND ECONOMIC FACTORS

Unemployment

Let's think now about some of the more practical issues that arise from the change in Dave's financial circumstances. (These relate specifically to the material covered in mandatory Unit 2.)

Imagine the following scene some weeks after Dave was made redundant.

Dave and Jenny were sitting quietly in the kitchen one evening, and the children were sleeping soundly upstairs. Dave picked up the evening paper and began to browse through it, turning the pages slowly until he came to the 'Jobs Vacant' section. 'What about this one?' exclaimed Dave, pushing the section of the paper across the table to Jenny.

'*Experienced Supervisor Required – Dalston Electrics*,' she read out loud. 'But that's ideal for you, Dave – exactly what you were doing before.' Jenny tried to hide the excitement in her voice. 'Let's write a letter of application right now,' she suggested. 'Hold on a minute,' said Dave thoughtfully. 'How would I get to Little Dalston without a car? There's no way I could get there on the bus.'

A frown flickered across Jenny's face. 'Well, you can drive. We'll have to get a car.' Dave tried to imagine life with a car of their own, thinking of the benefits and the freedom it would give them. 'But that would mean taking out a loan, Jenny. I don't expect that would be possible while we're on

'What an excellent idea, Miss Jones. Presumably it came from one of the men?'

State benefits.' 'Oh, that's a point,' she murmured.

They sat in silence for a minute or two, trying to think the problem through. 'Let's work out what we get each week and see if there is any chance of stretching our money a bit further,' Dave suggested. 'Okay, I'll get some paper and a pen,' said Jenny.

▌▌▶ **TASK** *Assessing income and expenses*
Jenny and Dave sat down together with a blank sheet of paper, drew a line across the page and wrote the headings *Income* and *Expenses*.

Income	£	p
Income support		_____
Family credit		_____
Housing benefit		_____
Milk tokens		_____
Child benefit:		_____
– Steve		_____
– Nick		_____
– Zoë		_____
Social services grant		_____
Other		_____
Total		_____

Expenses	£	p
Rent		_____
Council tax (after rebates)		_____
Water and sewage rates		_____
Household insurance		_____
Electricity		_____
Gas		_____
Telephone		_____
Food		_____
Milk/milk products		_____
TV licence		_____
Clothes		_____
Newspapers/magazines, etc.		_____
Transport		_____
Entertainment		_____
Other		_____
Total		_____

You have enough information about the family's circumstances to find out roughly how much they will receive each week, and how much their expenses are likely to be. Remember that they are in rented accommodation and will be eligible for housing benefit, so you will need to find out the average cost of renting the sort of terraced house described in the story.

To do this you will need to talk to someone you know who lives in a similar kind of house, preferably someone you know quite well who won't mind telling you the costs of such things as rent, council tax, and so on. This will be a good opportunity for you to practise the skill of talking with people about personal matters which they wouldn't want repeated to others in the community; you will only be given such information if you can be trusted to keep it confidential. (If you have any difficulty finding someone living in a house similar to the one in the story, ask your tutor for advice.) The costs of other items, such as food for Zoë, relate specifically to Dave and Jenny's family: you can find these out by visiting appropriate shops.

Make your calculations on a weekly basis, to find out what their expenses are, on average, each week. You can use this exercise as evidence of your ability to meet the performance criteria related to the core skills unit Application of Number (Elements 2.1 and 2.2).

The next thing is to decide whether Dave and Jenny have sufficient spare cash each week to afford the loan they would need in order to buy a car. Bear in mind that they must always look ahead and be ready for any unexpected emergencies, such as occurred when the boiler broke down.▪

✺ **OBSERVATIONS**
Jenny and Dave soon realise that their hopes of affording a loan are unrealistic.

Not surprisingly, Dave and Jenny were disappointed. They sat in silence for some time, keeping their thoughts to themselves. Finally Jenny broke the silence. 'Oh well,' she sighed, 'I'll have to try to get a part-time job in the supermarket again.' Dave nodded in agreement.▪

Sharing family responsibilities

Jenny's chances of finding part-time work are likely to be quite good. Nowadays women in our society make up a large proportion of the part-time workforce, and, before Jenny had Zoë she did part-time work. For Dave and Jenny, however, this change would require a careful look at the roles each of them currently play in the family. They would also need to check the effects any *earnings* might have on the level of *benefits* they already

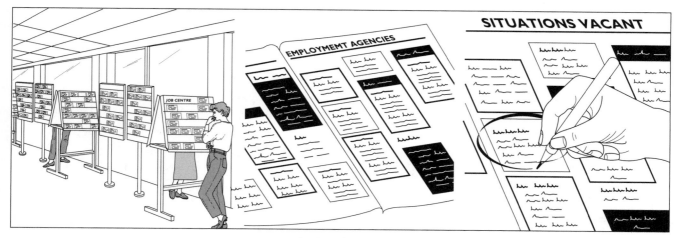

Looking for a job

receive as a family. What benefits would they lose if Jenny were to earn more than £40 per week? This can be checked quite easily; on the other hand, sorting out who will take on which family responsibilities if Jenny gets a job will take rather longer.

Having decided that it would be worth it, Dave and Jenny set about trying to identify the responsibilities each of them undertakes in and around the home. They come up with the following list.

- Childcare
  - washing and bathing
  - toileting and changing nappies
  - taking the children to school or playschool, and collecting them
  - clearing up and cleaning
  - putting the children to bed
  - reading a bedtime story
  - cooking
  - feeding the children
  - giving the night-time feed
  - going to the clinic
- Domestic
  - shopping
  - washing clothes
  - ironing
  - cleaning
  - vacuuming
  - dusting
  - changing bedding
- Maintenance
  - mending broken appliances
  - general DIY
  - cutting the lawn
  - gardening
- Additional
  - changing library books
  - paying bills

Until now Dave helped with the childcare jobs when he wasn't at work, but the childcare responsibilities have largely been Jenny's, as have all the domestic jobs, except for Dave's help with the shopping. The maintenance jobs have been Dave's responsibility; as an engineer he enjoys DIY work. Other jobs they shared.

TASK *Sharing roles and responsibilities*
There are lots of ways Jenny and Dave might decide to share out the jobs differently once Jenny is in work. Select four families with children, and identify how the responsibilities listed above are shared between the various members of the family, including the children. Try to include couples in which both partners are working and others in which one partner stays at home.

Remember what has been said about confidentiality, and the need to respect personal information. You should treat the people in your survey anonymously: their identity won't change the outcome of the survey.∎

OBSERVATIONS
You should have learned from this exercise that responsibilities within families are shared in a variety of ways, and for a variety of personal reasons. Families organise themselves according to what's best for them.

From this activity you should also have learned how to present your findings for your audience. Try to make sure that you meet all the performance criteria for the core skills units Communication (Element 2.2) and Information Technology (Element 2.3).∎

Having a home

If you have time, you may like to imagine how Jenny and Dave might have shared out their responsibilities had the need arisen. Of more importance to Jenny and Dave themselves at this stage, however, will be the fact that they do actually have a family home and household tasks to share out.

At times of disappointment there is usually *something* that we can be thankful for, so looking on the bright side of things can be a useful quality in the type of work you will be doing. In Dave and Jenny's case, the fact that they rent rather than own their home could be a blessing in disguise. If Jenny and Dave had decided to buy the terraced house when they had a regular income, they would now be in danger of not being able to maintain the **mortgage** repayments. This would mean that their home might be taken away from them, or **repossessed**. They would then have been homeless, and dependent upon the State to provide them either with accommodation or the necessary funds to pay for rented accommodation.

Being homeless

Homelessness has become a serious social issue in modern Britain. The voluntary organisation Shelter put the number of homeless in Britain in 1991 as high as 3 million. Many of these people belonged to families faced with similar circumstances to Jenny and Dave's. Official government statistics for the same year, which use a much narrower definition of homelessness, nevertheless show that 162 000 households were classified as homeless.

Homelessness brings both immediate and longer-term problems. The immediate problem is to secure alternative accommodation, which can be done either through the help and support of the social services or a local housing association, or by making personal arrangements through family or friends. The longer-term consequences of homelessness are more complex, depending on the particular circumstances of the people concerned. One likely outcome is the need to reorganise the family responsibilities if one or both parents can find work. Another, of course, is the acute emotional stress caused by the ongoing strain of the situation.

> ### TASK Temporary accommodation
> Suppose that Dave and Jenny had owned the terraced house, and are now faced with a repossession order because they can no longer meet the mortgage repayments. They have applied to the social services and a local housing association for permanent accommodation: none is immediately available, so they have been put on a waiting list. In the meantime they must find temporary accommodation. They could be faced with one of the following options:
>
> 1 They could move in with Dave's parents.
> 2 They could move into temporary council or housing association accommodation.
> 3 They might be placed by social services in bed-and-breakfast accommodation.
> 4 They could live temporarily in a family hostel.
> 5 Jenny and the children could be housed separately from Dave.

Jenny and Dave leave Hotspur Street

If you are unsure what is involved in choices 2–4, then get the necessary information from your tutors, or from the relevant social services and housing association literature. (Treat this as a 'finding out' task.) Remember that each of these choices is a short-term solution, but you don't know how temporary it will be.

It is preferable to undertake this task as a group activity rather than by yourself: you need to get as many views and perspectives on each alternative as you can. Also, we cannot assume that Dave and Jenny will agree on each choice or, worse still, that they will agree on the final decision. Such disagreements can add to the strain for people in this position, so it may be useful for you to have some of *your* own feelings challenged and perhaps even discounted.∎

> ### OBSERVATIONS
> It's likely that certain key principles or factors will have influenced your discussion and your decisions. One of the key factors to emerge should have been that of independence. In Britain it is usual for young families to want to live in their own home, and to be independent from their parents and the State. In other societies or cultures the traditions may be different from this and people may live as extended families, in communes or with their parents as a matter of course. Their children may be cared for by some of the family members, or by carers within their community. In Israel, for instance, babies and children who live in a kibbutz, a large agricultural commune, may be cared for collectively while their parents go to work. In a commune or kibbutz, all share the income from the work and there is no discrimination between levels of work or male/female roles. This system can work well, perhaps because the childcare provided in

the kibbutz is comparable to that which would be provided in a family home. These children become attached to a number of carers as well as to their parents.

In your discussions, the welfare of Nick, Steve and Zoë is likely to have been another key factor – indeed you may have seen this as the most significant factor of all, particularly as we don't know what Jenny and Dave's eventual solution will be. Staying with Dave's parents may well be the most appealing choice, causing the least emotional distress and upheaval to the children, especially Steve.■

CHILDREN'S NEEDS

Childcare

Childcare is an important factor when assessing family needs. As long as either Dave or Jenny is employed, but not both, the well-being of the children poses no real problem. Were both to find work, however, even on a part-time basis, the situation would be very different – as with a one-parent family in which the parent goes out to work.

Let's suppose that Dave and Jenny prove lucky and both find work. Childcare now becomes an issue. The first thing they will need to know is what childcare facilities are available near Hotspur Street. There are a number of possibilities:

- a childminder;
- a local authority day nursery;
- a private day nursery;
- a playgroup, an after-school club, or a family centre;
- a nursery nurse or nanny in the home.

▸ TASK Identifying childcare facilities
Begin by making sure that you know what is provided by each of the services listed above. Then find out:

1 Which of the services are provided free.
2 The roles and responsibilities of the local authority in the provision of these services.
3 The cost (if any) of these services (either per hour, per session or per week).

✷ OBSERVATIONS
Two things should have emerged in your findings. Firstly, the prominent part now played by **childminders** in the provision of childcare, and secondly, the comparatively high cost of the childcare services if used extensively.

Most childminders care for children within their own homes, often because this role is mainly carried out by women with young children of their own. Your research may have revealed that social services departments keep a **register of childminders**. This register is important in that it tries to ensure the protection and well-being of young children. If you don't already know, find out what is required before a person can become a registered childminder.

Your research should also have revealed that making use of the childcare services can be a costly business. Dave and Jenny, for example, will have to think very carefully about the amount of time they spend at work in relation to the cost of the childcare needed to support their combined absences from home. This is not just a financial issue. There is a very fine balance between the demands and responsibilities of parenthood and the financial needs of the family.

Children as individuals

Children's rights and protection were the subject of government legislation in the Children Act 1989. You should already be familiar with this Act, which provides a framework for the care and protection of children.

A number of agencies and organisations have specific responsibilities for children's welfare. Some of these are mentioned below as we consider some of the key areas in which children's emotional and physical well-being may be at risk. Again, it is up to you to find out for yourself any further information you need.

Child abuse

In this country it is a criminal offence to abuse children, yet sadly we all too frequently read of cases of child abuse. The local authorities, through the social services, have a particular responsibility to treat the welfare of children as of paramount importance. They usually classify child abuse into four categories:

- neglect;
- physical abuse;
- emotional abuse;
- sexual abuse.

All are serious, and all are difficult to identify – often the abuse has taken place some time before the signs of it are fully evident. It is particularly difficult to protect children when the abusers are members of their own family, or others close to the children. Social services have the power to take action where they believe a child is at risk. This can mean removing the child from his or her family and placing the child in care. Such drastic action is taken only as a last resort.

Preventing the occurrence of abuse is the aim of all concerned. Those with a professional responsibility, such as doctors, nurses, social workers and teachers, are trained to spot signs of neglect or physical abuse, or both. Everyone must be alert to the dangers that children face. Bruises, failure to thrive, skin burns or cuts and any radical changes in a child's behaviour are all signs to watch out for. Also helpful is the **register for non-accidental injuries** which is kept by each local authority social services department. This records children's injuries where there are doubts about the circumstances in which the injuries occurred. More often than not, however, it's people in the community who first raise the alarm when things are not as they ought to be with children they know who live close by. Professional services always depend upon close and effective links with the community.

Grief and separation

Though we have legislation to protect children, their immediate welfare is protected by those with direct responsibility for them – parents at home, teachers at school, playworkers at clubs and recreation centres, and so on. For the children it's people, not laws, in whom they must place their confidence and trust. When they experience pain or sadness, it is to those closest to them that they look for comfort and support. For example, children who experience bereavement need adults who can help them through the stages of mourning that will follow, especially if the person who has died was someone very close to them. At such moments children are vulnerable, and likely to suffer emotional and psychological reactions.

Imagine the following situation. Nine-year-old David challenges his grandmother to a running race. He wins the race and his grandmother laughingly pants,

Young people often need emotional support

'You'll be the death of me, young man, I'm far too old for this sort of thing.' Three weeks later, the grandmother dies of a heart attack. The whole family are shocked and sad, but accept that this was not unexpected after a long history of heart disease. David, in contrast, knows nothing of his grandmother's medical history and believes he may be directly responsible for his grandmother's death.

This story may be an extreme example, but children coping with profound sadness do need very special understanding. To postpone or deny grief, or to try to cover up strong feelings, can be very damaging and may have lasting effects. Dealing with childhood grief is a very specialised area of social care, and fortunately it is quite rare in this country for children while very young to lose a parent. All care workers, however, will at some stage in their career have to use their training and skills to help in the care of the dying and to support bereaved family members.

Children are also emotionally and psychologically at risk when faced with the break-up of their family through separation or divorce. Though children are often good at hiding their distress, this doesn't mean that they are not affected. Indeed, younger children may even think they are responsible for their parent's separation, and feel guilty about it.

Children in need: voluntary organisations

In addition to the support and protection provided by the social services, a number of voluntary agencies are specifically concerned with children's welfare. Such organisations often work closely with the social services, and have become increasingly important as a source of childcare support.

Many of these organisations, most of which have charitable status, have been in existence for many years now. The best known is The National Society for the Prevention of Cruelty to Children (NSPCC), which was established in 1884 in response to the needs of children who were suffering hardship and ill-treatment in the factories and towns of Victorian England. Another important organisation is Childline, which offers a free and confidential telephone service to children who feel in need of protection.

 TASK *Voluntary organisations for children*
Find out the following:

- where your local NSPCC is situated;
- how it is funded;
- how it links with social services;
- what support it offers to children and their parents;
- the responsibilities of the voluntary workers;
- the responsibilities of the paid employees;

- the telephone number of Childline;
- the procedures to be followed by Childline staff when a call is received.∎

Children with special needs

Some children, such as Jane in the story, have very special needs. As you know, Jane has Down's syndrome, a congenital disorder present since birth. The incidence of Down's syndrome is about 1 in 700 live births: affected children have 47 chromosomes instead of the normal 46. Screening procedures in pregnancy can now identify certain congenital conditions. If you have investigated the specialist services offered at health centres, you may have heard the term **amniocentesis.** This test is now widely available to women who are at risk of having children with Down's syndrome.

Down's syndrome is only one of several congenital disorders you may learn about on the GNVQ course. Congenital dislocation of the hip, congenital heart disease, cystic fibrosis and congenital cataracts are all disorders present at birth. They are not necessarily, however, genetic in origin. With the help and guidance of your tutors, make sure that you are aware of the effects of each of these disorders.

 TASK Down's syndrome
Find out:

- the physical characteristics and effects of Down's syndrome;
- how an amniocentesis test is carried out, and whether the test is available to all pregnant women.∎

Special needs: schooling

During her childhood Jane will have particular rights and entitlements, for example in relation to her schooling. She has the right to attend the same primary school as any other child of her age in the community, and will receive special help and support in primary school if she does so. Alternatively, she has the option of attending a special school or unit which caters for children with special educational needs.

 TASK Special educational needs
Find out:

- Jane's educational entitlements from the age of 3 until the age of 21;
- the help she can expect to receive in an ordinary primary school classroom;
- the difference between a special school and a unit for children with special needs in an ordinary primary school;

- the schools or units in your area for children with special learning needs.∎

Special needs: choices to be made

For Jane, as for many in her position, choices are available and so some very difficult decisions must be made. Whether she attends a special school or an ordinary school is one such choice; whether when she's older she lives at home or in care is another. Such complex decisions depend on many factors. Much will depend on the physical extent of her disabilities, her intellectual ability, and her confidence about coping in an ordinary classroom. Also relevant will be her need for specialist treatment, and whether her parents are in a position to help and support her.

Behind these immediate practical issues may lie difficult *moral* issues. If Jane is put into a special school, for example, is she being denied certain basic opportunities in life? Alternatively, if she is placed in an ordinary school, is she being denied specialist support? Likewise, whether she remains at home or lives in care will raise similar moral issues when this difficult decision has to be made.

Because she belongs to a minority group, Jane is subject to the kind of discrimination experienced by members of other minority groups. Where children are involved, discriminatory behaviour, such as bullying, can often be the result simply of childish ignorance and misunderstanding. Nevertheless, it's hurtful and distressing to those who suffer it.

 TASK Considering moral issues
Assessing Jane's needs is a complex process because of the variety and sensitivity of many of the issues involved. This is no reason for looking the other way, however: this is the reality for people in Jane's position.

This task focuses on some of the moral issues under-lying the decisions that will have to be made about Jane. It should be carried out within a group, and with the help and guidance of your tutors.

- Identify some of the advantages and disadvantages if Jane attends a primary school.
- Identify some of the advantages and disadvantages for Jane of going to a special learning unit.
- Identify some of the forms of discrimination Jane may experience as a young person. Should we excuse children who discriminate against people like Jane, on the grounds that they don't know any better?
- Identify some of the forms of discrimination Jane may have to face as an adult. Is it possible to have equal opportunity for everyone?∎

A lot of ground has been covered since we constructed a possible job description for a care worker (Chapter 3). What was outlined there was a very general idea of the abilities and experience required of a care professional. As we've worked through the duties and responsibilities associated with the job, a more detailed picture has emerged of the kinds of skills and understandings involved. This section offers a reminder of the most important of these.

Respect for the individual

Respect for the individual is at the heart of caring. Everyone has rights, whether they be legal rights or simply expectations. Respecting people's beliefs, opinions, backgrounds and personal freedom is vital. Even when people lose the ability to look after themselves fully, it's your job to see that they achieve as much independence as possible, to help them retain their dignity and self-respect. Caring for people also means understanding their dependence on, and membership of, different groups, and respecting their individuality as members of these groups. Taking a positive attitude towards individuals who, for one reason or another, are different from the majority of people is an essential part of your responsibilities both to clients and to society.

Confidentiality

Respect for the individual also means respect for their privacy. You will often have access to very personal information about clients; it's your responsibility to make sure that this is treated sensitively. Sometimes other professionals need certain information in order to carry out their part of a care plan, but you mustn't give them information that they don't need. Where personal information is to be shared with others, the client should be informed and the matter talked through with them.

Trust

Respecting people's privacy is important in helping to develop trust, and trust is vital in developing effective working relationships. Good relationships with clients are crucial, but so are good relationships with other members of the care team, with members of the client's family, with friends and neighbours, and with any specialist agencies involved.

Teamwork and relationships

You are part of a team, all the members of which need to trust each other. But good teamwork is more than just getting on with each other; it also involves knowing and understanding each other's roles and responsibilities, and trusting each other's skills and judgements. Caring is organised around the principle of teamwork. Working in and with the community is an essential aspect of teamwork in action, and many of the health and care services to support those in need are focused on the community.

Care plan

Care plans are a central feature in assessing and meeting clients' needs. They may be formally or informally constructed, and will usually involve a team of people both in the planning of care and in the delivery of care. In care plans for which you are responsible, it will be your job to ensure that all those supporting the care plan understand their roles as members of the team.

Care planning: identifying and assessing need

Effective care plans depend on the care professional having the knowledge and skills to identify and assess the clients' needs. This applies just as much to the practical things associated with care as to the specialist health-care knowledge that is required. In making judgements and decisions about the client's circumstances and needs, you need to understand the broader social and economic factors which may affect his or her well-being.

Collecting, storing and using information

Making decisions about other people's lives involves collecting, storing and using information about them. As well as observing confidentiality, you need to know where to obtain information, how to store it, and who has the right to use it. You must also keep the information up to date, and in a form that can be understood by others who have to use it.

Compiling and storing records involves different systems and skills. If you use a computerised record-keeping system, remember that you are legally required by the **Data Protection Act 1984** to register the fact you are storing such information.

Communicating

Communication is at the centre of caring. It is what people spend most of their time doing. As a care worker you will be involved daily in face-to-face contact with clients, in telephoning, keeping records, explaining care plans, and giving instructions – as well as dozens of other everyday matters. All of these require good, practical communication skills, especially writing and oral skills.

But communication has other important functions also. *How* you communicate will be just as significant as *what* you communicate. This, too, requires skill. To develop relationships based on confidence, respect and trust requires forms of communication beyond words: you will need the gestures, facial expressions, eye contact, body language and other signals that convey your interest, sympathy, encouragement and respect for other people.

Listening and observing

Communication is a two-way process: you need the skills that will help others to communicate with you. This means knowing when to listen and observe, respecting and valuing the information, opinions and feelings of others. Often people understand their own needs better than you do, but need time and attention to communicate these successfully to you.■

KEY WORDS AND TECHNICAL TERMS

Cataract A condition of the eye in which the lens or its capsule is clouded. Cataracts may be congenital or develop as a result of disease or old age.

Charitable organisations Organisations which rely for their existence on money raised from the public, and which rely also on the work of volunteers to provide the services they offer.

Child benefit A weekly allowance paid to parents for each of their children up to the age of 16, or up to the age of 19 if the child remains in full-time education.

Commune A small community in which members share a close and supportive relationship with each other.

Culture A group or community of people with shared beliefs, customs and practices. Modern societies are often made up of a diversity of different cultural groups, as in Britain today.

Cystic fibrosis An inherited condition present at birth in which glands produce thick mucus which affects the person's breathing and digestion.

Diversity Variety – lots of differences. Thus, a patchwork quilt can be made of a variety of pieces, each different from the others.

Equality of opportunity The principle that everyone should have an equal chance to benefit from the opportunities available, whether educational, economic or social. These opportunities should be available to everyone, irrespective of race, gender or disability. Thus Jane, for example, should not be denied the opportunity to attend her local primary school because of her condition.

Family The basic social unit in society. Families can take many different forms, including nuclear families, extended families, and single-parent families.

Family credit Financial assistance paid by the Department of Social Security to people in work who have dependent children and whose income is below a certain level. The amount of money they receive is dependent upon the size of the family, the ages of the children, and the amount of earned income.

Hostel A place offering accommodation to people with varying needs. For example, hostels may be for people who would otherwise be homeless, for women suffering violence from their partners, or for people with mental health problems.

Housing association A voluntary organisation that provides rented accommodation for people who would otherwise have nowhere to live.

Housing benefit Financial assistance paid to people on low incomes or no income to assist them in paying their rent or mortgage.

Income support A welfare benefit paid to people over 18 years of age (except in certain circumstances) who are not working full-time and who have an income below a level set by the Government. Those entitled to claim this benefit include the unemployed, those partially employed but earning less than the Government limit, and older people and lone parents whose income does not exceed the Government limit.

Labelling The process by which people are identified not as individuals but according to a groups they belong to. Thus people are labelled as students (yourself), unemployed (Dave), elderly (Bob, Cath and Tom), adolescents, and so on. Labelling is often linked with prejudice.

Moral issues Issues in which decisions must be taken which will have crucial effects on other people's lives. For example, decisions about Jane's education may be critical for her future: the choices facing her relatives are enormously difficult, and there are no simple right or wrong answers.

Mortgage A loan to buy a house, repaid to the building society or bank from which the money has been borrowed.

Norm The standard observed by a majority of people in regard to a particular situation, behaviour or circumstance. Most of us accept certain rules or norms of behaviour as a natural part of our lives. Some of these rules are formalised as laws, so that everyone is clear about what is acceptable and what is not.

Prejudice An opinion formed about someone or something which is based not on the evidence available but on assumptions. Thus, if people jump to conclusions about Dave just because he is unemployed, that is prejudice.

Primary socialisation The process by which young children learn about and come to accept the world around them and their roles within it. This is an important stage in their development: during this period they are greatly influenced by the models of behaviour, and the values of those close to them (see *role modelling*, below).

Register for non-accidental injuries A record of children 'at risk' kept by the child protection officer in the social services department. It records the names of children who have been abused, or who are suspected of having been abused.

Repossession The loss of your home when you are unable to pay your mortgage. The building society or bank which gave you the mortgage may sell your home in order to pay your debt.

Role modelling Presenting attitudes and models of behaviour for others to imitate and follow. It is particularly important that young children are presented with good role models.

Self-esteem The way we see and feel about ourselves. Feeling good about ourselves helps to give us self-respect, personal self-worth, and a purpose in life. It is a crucial part of our emotional well-being.

Social classification The categorising of people into social groups on the basis of their occupation. The Government uses social classification statistics as a means of showing changes in the social patterns and trends in British society.

Stereotyping The process by which the labels given to people are then associated with particular values, usually negative ones. Dave, for example, may first be labelled as unemployed, and may then be represented as someone who prefers to live off State benefits because he is lazy and irresponsible. This fits the stereotypical view of the unemployed.

Values The beliefs that we have about what is acceptable and what is not, what is right and what is wrong. Values provide the basis for defining the norms in the family, the community and society. They are views about our behaviour and responsibilities as citizens and people.

Welfare benefits Financial benefits paid by the Department of Social Security to people who are unable to support themselves. Typical reasons are that they are homeless, ill or unemployed.

7 • The care services and promoting health

This chapter looks at national and local provision of health and care services, and at health promotion. In this chapter you will:

- be introduced to the organisation and structure of the health and care services and look at their place and role within the welfare state;
- find out about some of the key health and care services provided within the community;
- be introduced to the general aims of health promotion, and be made aware of the care worker's responsibilities as a promoter of health;
- be made aware of the importance of caring for your own well-being.

A number of community care services have already been identified in relation to the particular needs of some of the people living in Hotspur Street. This chapter shows you how these local services link into the national arrangements for health and care provision, together with a brief outline of how society's ideas about community care have influenced the changes that have taken place over the years. None of this is covered in depth as there are many textbooks on the subject.

Health promotion receives much the same kind of treatment. It is a vast topic in its own right, and all we shall look at here are its general aims and some of the key issues that it raises for you as a care worker.

BEING A RESOURCE FOR OTHERS

As a health care worker, you need to know about the health and care services because many of the people you will meet may well seek your professional advice and guidance on the matter. They will want to know what services exist and what services they are entitled to. As a professional you may also be expected to know something about their origins and development.

THE HISTORY OF THE WELFARE STATE

In 1942 the **Beveridge Report** argued that it was the duty of the Government to put an end to *disease*, *ignorance*, *squalor*, *unemployment* and *poverty* in Britain. In 1945, as the victorious troops came home from the Second World War, there was the added feeling that all sections of British society had the right to look forward to a better future.

By 1948 this report had given rise to a series of Acts of Parliament which together provided the basis for what has been known ever since as the **welfare state**. The fundamental idea was that every citizen of Britain had the right to benefit from good health, a good education, a job, a home, and a reasonable standard of living. In the case of health care and education, these had to be provided free of charge, since an enormous section of the population would otherwise have been denied them. This was the Britain that Bob returned to when he started out on his new life with Cath in Hotspur Street at the end of the war.

To see how the welfare state developed, we need to go back to the 19th century. As people moved from the countryside into the towns and cities in search of work in the new manufacturing industries that were rapidly springing up, the problems of homelessness, crime and ill health grew on a scale hitherto

Airmen returning from a mission during the Second World War

Workhouse for the poor and destitute in Victorian London

unknown. If you've seen the film *Oliver*, which is based on Charles Dickens' novel about the life of Oliver Twist, you will have a very vivid picture of what life was like for thousands of people living in Victorian London.

Such distressing social conditions were soon accepted as inevitable, and the people who became ill or homeless or who fell on hard times were seen as having only themselves to blame. Attempts to solve these problems provide the background to a century of steady progress towards the ideal of the welfare state. It proved to be a long and difficult journey, partly because many of those in authority felt that the social welfare of the mass of the population was not the responsibility of the State. Failure to cope, for whatever reason, was the fault of those concerned, they thought: they should not expect sympathy and help from the State. As burdens on society, they should be treated with as little respect for their human dignity as possible. It was the responsibility of their families to provide for their welfare. Where this did not happen they could expect little public mercy: they now fell victim to the Victorian's version of community care.

The idea of community responsibility for those in need dates back to the reign of Queen Elizabeth I. Then it was the community that had to support the sick, the poor and the unemployed from taxes raised in the local villages and towns. The Victorians took these arrangements a step further by building large institutions, known as workhouses, in which to house such people. Though originally intended to be places for the poor and the homeless within the local community, all too soon, they became places where the rest of society's problems could be locked away: the mentally ill, criminals, and those unable to work, as well as the destitute and their families. Very quickly many of them became little more than asylums or prisons and were referred to as 'houses of correction'.

The workhouse serves as a powerful reminder of Victorian attitudes towards social welfare and towards people who were unable to look after themselves. The idea that many of society's social problems can be shut away in institutions is one that has remained with us until very recently. For many people in Victorian Britain, life inside the institution was no better than the squalor and wretchedness of the life outside that they had left behind. For some, notably children, it was the only life they knew, until early adulthood. Such was the fate of the young Oliver Twist, whose first taste of life was experienced in a workhouse under the brutal regime of the fearsome Mr Bumble.

The story of the welfare state is about how these attitudes were challenged and steadily replaced by a view that the State, as well as the family and the individual, has a part to play in providing for the basic needs and care of each of its citizens. Progress towards this goal owed a great deal to the hard work and single-mindedness of a few men and women. Many of them belonged to the Church; others came from different sections of society. Most Victorian schools, hospitals, homes for the poor and workhouses were established and paid for either by families living within the community, or by the Church. These were known as 'charities'.

Alongside the work of the charities there emerged a feeling among some political leaders of the time that change was necessary. The result was a steady stream of Parliamentary legislation in the late 19th and early 20th centuries, concerning aspects of health, education and social welfare. Often this was in the face of bitter opposition. One drawback of these efforts, however, was that they clung to the idea that people should contribute towards the cost of these services. Schools, for example, were not free, so although the fees were low, the very poor could still not afford an education. Beveridge's triumph was in successfully challenging this basic assumption, and thereby establishing the guiding principle of the welfare state: that people had rights and benefits as citizens of Britain.

TASK The welfare state

Find out something about each of the following, and as you do so, pick out the issues and arguments that each raises in terms of changing attitudes towards social welfare.

- *Friendly Societies* What were they, and how did they function?
- *Charity Schools* Who were they for, and how were they run?
- *The National Insurance Act 1911* What did it provide? Who was eligible to benefit from it, and who was not?
- *National Assistance* What was it, and when was it introduced? What is it known as today?∎

OBSERVATIONS

From your research you should have found that many of the issues and arguments that influenced Victorian attitudes regarding health and social welfare are still prominent today. Who should take responsibility for providing care, who should pay for it, and where those in need of help should receive care – these are all key issues in the thinking behind the NHS and Community Care Act 1990. These are

issues that you need to keep at the front of your mind as you read through the next few sections of this chapter.

One final thought on our Victorian heritage. You may have discovered just how close the past can be to the health and care services of today when you realise that a great many of our older hospitals and residential and nursing homes are based in old Victorian workhouses. Are there any in your locality?∎

THE ORGANISATION OF THE WELFARE STATE

Putting into practice the policies and ideals of Beveridge's welfare state has been the work of a number of large government departments, shown in the table below. As you look through the table, think how each department relates to Beveridge's plan to eliminate disease, ignorance, squalor, unemployment and poverty in postwar Britain. Fill in one or other of these social conditions related to each department's responsibilities.

Government department	Responsibilities	Related social condition
Health (DoH)	National Health Service, social services	
Social Security (DSS)	Welfare benefits	
Education (DfE)	Schools, higher education and further education	
Employment (DE)	Employment and training	
Environment (DoE)	Housing and environmental issues	

Other government departments also have responsibilities for matters related to health and social welfare. The Home Office, for example, has responsibility for immigration issues, race relations and the probation service.

As far as your professional needs are concerned, the major provider of health and care services is the Department of Health. The education service has an important role to play, but not an extensive one. It provides for the educational needs of children such as Jane, and for children with special needs generally. Local education authorities also employ educational psychologists to support the needs of children with particular learning problems. They may provide pre-school facilities, too, of which children such as Steve could take advantage.

Caring services or care industry?

The health and care services are often referred to as 'the caring services'; sometimes they are referred to as 'the care industry'. Both names tell us something important about them. The first title reflects their primary aim, to provide care to those who need it. Whether the carers are doctors, social workers, chiropodists, ambulance workers or whoever, they see their first responsibility as being to the client. When you realise, however, that in order to perform their jobs they are supported by literally millions of people you get some idea of why the services are occasionally referred to as the care industry. The National Health Service (NHS) is the single largest employer in the whole of western Europe, and spends billions of pounds each year. Many of these people are employed by the Department of Health. Like any other business or industry with a huge workforce and a vast budget, its operation and administration have to be carefully organised and managed. The NHS operates at three administrative levels: central, regional, and local. We shall be concerned with two aspects of the Department of Health's organisation and its operations, the NHS and the social services. Although each adopts a pattern of central, regional and local administration, there are clear differences between them. Whilst the main focus will be on local administration and practice, it is important that you have some grasp of how the system functions as a whole.

The National Health Service

The National Health Service was established in 1948 as the centrepiece in the new welfare state. It has been reorganised on a number of occasions since then, the latest reorganisation having taken place quite recently; this time changes have been mainly to do with the way that the service is funded. Further reference will be made to this development in a later section of the chapter.

The diagram provides an outline of how the NHS in England is currently structured for administrative purposes. Wales, Scotland and Northern Ireland each have a different organisational structure. The organisation of the health services in Wales is similar to that for England, except that there are no Regional Health Authorities, only District Health Authorities. In Scotland the system is the responsibility of the Secretary of State for Scotland, who administers the service through a Scottish Home and Health Department and a series of district Health Boards. In

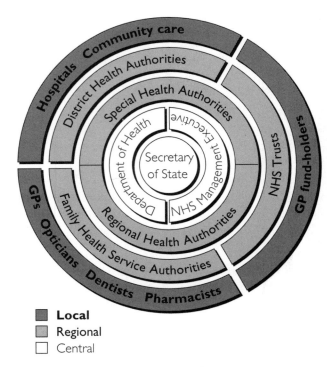

Local
Regional
Central

Organisation of the NHS in England

Northern Ireland the health services are administered alongside the social services through four Health Boards, which are directly resourced and answerable to the Department of Health in England.

Primary health care

We shall focus on the local end of the system, because that is where you will work as part of a team of community-based professionals. The services these people provide are known as the **primary health services**: they represent the first point of direct contact between the client and those responsible for providing care, treatment or advice. These services, including the provision for acute care and mental health care, are organised either by the **District Health Authority (DHA)** or by the **Family Health Service Authority (FHSA)**, both of which are regionally based.

By far the most widely used of the primary health services is the local **general practitioner (GP)**. As a result, the work of GPs has become a focus for the development of local **primary health care teams**, sometimes based in GPs' surgeries, but more often in a local **health centre**. The team usually consists of the GP, the local practice nurse, the district nurse, the community midwife, the health visitor and the community psychiatric nurse. Such teams provide access to a large group of community-based professionals whose work is organised and co-ordinated to meet the health needs of the community.

The primary health care services also include local dentists, opticians and pharmacists. Like the GPs, the dentists and opticians have patient registers, and you register with them in the same way as you would with a doctor. Besides their role as first-line providers of treatment, they also offer advice in the form of periodic check-ups, regardless of whether treatment may be needed.

The diagram below identifies the key people in the local primary health care services. But keep in mind that they do not operate in isolation – they work as a team, closely linked into the services provided by the other community-based professionals.

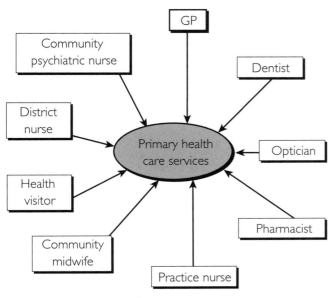

Local primary-health-care team

iiii▶ **TASK** *Primary health care*
Some of the services and professionals mentioned so far in this chapter may be new to you; others you will have found out about already, perhaps when assessing Tom's needs.

If you are going to work in the community, it's important that you know what services are available, what their responsibilities are, where they are located, and the roles of the people working in them. Complete the tasks set out below. Use any previous work that you may have done. Make sure that you follow your college or school's policy when asking for information from outside agencies. Remember that you are more likely to get a positive response from an organisation if the requests are carefully co-ordinated and organised on behalf of all of the members of the GNVQ group.

1 Find out from your nearest health centre what primary health care services it offers. What services would be available for Zoë?
2 Provide a brief outline of the role of each of the professionals and services identified in the primary health care diagram.
3 Find out where your local Family Health Service Authority is based. What are its responsibilities?
4 Find out where your District Health Authority is

based. Obtain the address, and request information about its responsibilities and the services it offers.

The social services

As was observed earlier, the social services have a different administrative structure from the NHS. Like the NHS, however, they have three levels of operation. The diagram shows how they are organised in England and Wales. The situations in Scotland and Northern Ireland are slightly different: in Scotland the social services are administered through Regional Local Authorities; in Northern Ireland they are administered, as we have just seen, alongside the health services through Health Boards.

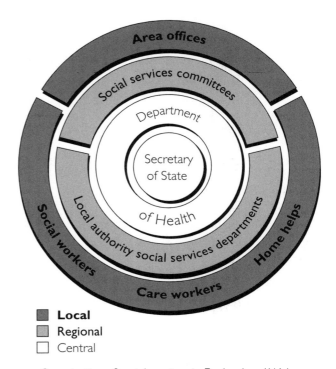

■ Local
■ Regional
□ Central

Organisation of social services in England and Wales

The key administrative units in the provision of community care in England and Wales are the regionally-based **local authority social services departments**. There is no equivalent in the social services of the community-based primary health care team. As a care worker, you will be part of the social services team responsible for providing a wide range of community services in your area. These services are run by a team manager from the local authority, who in turn is responsible to a local authority social services committee. Unlike the NHS, the pattern of regional organisation varies very considerably between local authorities: some divide their services one way, others another. Nevertheless, whatever groupings they adopt, they all provide services for:

• children and families;
• the elderly;
• people with physical disabilities or illnesses;
• people with mental health problems.

TASK Social services
As with the NHS, it's useful to know where and how you as a care worker fit into the system. Obtain the following information about your local authority social services department.

- How is the department structured?
- Does the department have area offices? If so, what role do they play?
- How many home-care workers, residential care workers, and social workers does the department employ?
- How many people over 80 years of age are living independently in their own homes with support from the local authority?
- What does it costs to keep a person in a residential care home for one week?
- How is the department funded?

FUNDING HEALTH AND CARE SERVICES

One of the biggest challenges facing any government at the moment is how to pay for the services that people are demanding. For a number of years the demand for health and care services has been far greater than the funds available to pay for them. Solving this problem is not easy, as the task below aims to show.

TASK Allocating funds
Imagine the following situation:

Bob has returned home and is being cared for by Cath. He does well for three weeks, but then suffers a sudden heart attack and requires major heart surgery. At the time of his earlier illness he had been advised to give up smoking, but had not managed to do so.

Morag, a 55-year old widow, is on the waiting list at the same hospital. She is due to have a heart-bypass operation on the day after Bob is admitted. Unfortunately the hospital has insufficient NHS funds at this time to perform both operations.

Now imagine that your GNVQ group is the hospital management team responsible for deciding what action to take. You have to come up with at least *five* possible options. By all means identify a preferred option if you wish, but you will probably find that you cannot finally decide which option to take without further information.

This task can be undertaken either as a discussion or as a simulation or role-play. If you want to try a simulation, get your tutor to help you set it up. Either way, the observations section below will provide you with some useful starting-points, so read it through first.∎

OBSERVATIONS
Since shortage of money is the problem, one obvious solution would be to find some other means of paying for one or both of the operations. Could the patients themselves pay? If this is not possible, or not felt to be appropriate, another way forward might be to try to choose which patient has the best claim and make one of them wait – but which one, and on what basis? If, in the team's view, the original spirit of Beveridge's welfare state (that everyone has an equal right to the benefits of health care) is important, then the money might have to be found from elsewhere in the hospital. But where from, and what might the effect be?

The point of the exercise, of course, is to start you thinking about how the health and care needs of the population can best be met when the funds for achieving this are limited.∎

Paying for health and social care

As should have emerged from your discussions, the cost of health and social care is met in a variety of ways. These are based on two main assumptions: firstly, that it is perfectly reasonable to require people who can afford it to contribute something towards the cost of their own treatment or care; and secondly, that people should be encouraged to see health care and social welfare as an essential part of their own responsibilities, and not just the responsibility of the government.

Both of these assumptions have helped to influence present government policy and practice. In 1948 all the health and care services were provided free of charge. This is no longer true: most people now are required at the point of use to pay something towards the cost of a number of the services they receive.

TASK Funding health and social care
When you were assessing Bob's needs you will have noted that in certain circumstances particular groups of people still receive these services free. One such group is children. Find out which services are free to children.

Some people are prepared to pay the whole cost for key services that they personally use, or alternatively, to pay into an insurance plan so that they can be treated privately should the need arise. Had either Bob or Morag been in a position to do this, it would have provided a possible solution to their problem. Find out how medical insurance works, and what services it offers.

Keeping the costs down by making the system more financially efficient has been a key aim of the Government's recent reorganisation of the NHS and of community care. You should by now know something about these changes from your work on the tasks in this and previous chapters. You should be familiar, for example, with such terms as *purchasers* and *providers*, *trust hospitals*, and *budget-holding GPs*. Check that you know, in outline, what each of these terms means, and that you understand how the funding process works. Your tutors may need to help you with this task as part of your study of mandatory Unit 3, Element 3.1.

Spreading the cost

A further aim of the new arrangements has been to encourage people to provide their own services, rather than rely upon those of the State. Behind this idea lies the re-establishment of charities and voluntary agencies as an essential feature of the health and care services. Thus the health and care services are provided from three main sources: the Government, the voluntary and charitable organisations, and through private bodies and individuals. In Unit 3, Element 3.1, you will find these referred to as the *statutory*, *non-statutory* and *independent* sectors.

Statutory sector

This consists of the NHS and the social services, which have been established by Parliament and are fully funded by central government.

Non-statutory sector

The voluntary sector is a little more complicated. In Britain today there are about 350 000 voluntary organisations providing health and social care services alongside the statutory organisations. They are all charitable organisations, depending for their existence on public donations and voluntary workers. However, because the government recognises them as an essential part of the system as a whole, many of them are now supported by government money. Many, too, are staffed by paid employees.

As a care worker you will have close links with many of these organisations, and will come to value their contributions highly. As we've seen, they have developed from a long and successful tradition of organisations providing care and support for those in need. We noted the establishment of the NSPCC in 1884; Dr Barnardo's dates from the same period (1866), and we could identify many more. If you have time, find out which of the others that are well known today came into existence in the last century, some perhaps under a different name.

Voluntary organisations have thus become a central part of the government's plans for the health and care services. When you look at the Community Care Act,

notice how dependent the Act's arrangements are upon the existence and support of these organisations. They have taken their place alongside the statutory agencies as **care service providers**. Their importance in community care is reflected in the setting up of a national body to co-ordinate them, the **National Council for Voluntary Organisations** (**NCVO**), which operates through local or community bodies called **Councils for Voluntary Services** (**CVS**). Make sure that you know where your local CVS is, what information it provides, and how it co-ordinates the community care services locally.

▌▶ TASK Non-statutory organisations

Choose *one* local voluntary organisation in which you have an interest, and obtain the following information about it.

- Who uses the service or facility?
- What are its main functions as an organisation?
- How is the organisation funded?
- Does it use paid employees?
- How many workers are unpaid volunteers?
- Are the users involved in the running of the organisation?▌

Private organisations

The independent sector provides health and care services which are paid for by the client. Most of these services are provided through profit-making organisations. Like the voluntary organisations, they were well established in the Victorian period. With the introduction of the welfare state it was confidently assumed that they would no longer be needed, but for the reasons described above this proved not to be the case. As with the voluntary organisations they have re-emerged as an important part of the Government's plans for meeting the growing demands for health and care services.

Over half a million operations each year are performed privately, and private nursing homes and residential homes are an increasing feature of the community health and care services. One indication of the growth in the private health care sector is that in 1992 over 2 million people were paying insurance premiums entitling them to various forms of private health care treatment. This sector also includes self-employed individuals, who charge for their services.

THE INVISIBLE CARERS

A further, all too often neglected, group of care providers help to keep the system going: the families, neighbours and friends of those needing care. As was observed earlier, a basic assumption underlying current thinking is that people should be more responsible for their own welfare. Community care has developed from this principle. In Britain today over 6 million people are providing care for the sick, the elderly, and those with disabilities. Only a very small proportion of those receiving such care are being supported through the statutory or voluntary services. Their care needs will be provided for by their families, neighbours and friends. Charity, as they say, begins at home.

It's easy to take the work and the dedication of such carers for granted, which is why they often seem so invisible and why their contributions go unrecognised. Think back to Bob's assessment and the care plan that was prepared for him: Cath, as his home carer, is expected to play a vital role in his rehabilitation programme. Always bear in mind that without people like Cath, community care would be completely unworkable.

COMMUNITY CARE

Having looked at the various pieces, we can now reassemble them in order to see the complete picture of community care. It is a complex arrangement, within which work a variety of people, some as part of statutory organisations, some on a voluntary basis, and others as members of privately run agencies. Yet others contribute as ordinary caring individuals.

The relationship between these people and the various organisations can be quite confusing, as can the way that they are administered and funded. The diagram below illustrates the range of health and care services that you would expect to find within a community setting.

Remember: at the point of contact with the client, caring is about individuals, not about services. Some people may never need to use any of these services; others may need several of them during their lifetime. The services are available, however, as and when needed.

▐▐▐➡ TASK Services available

The subjects for this task are Tom, Bob, Jane, Steve and Zoë. You now know quite a lot about each of them, about their personal circumstances as well as their age and states of health. You know, for example, that Tom is elderly, that he is showing signs of mental illness, and that he has no one to look after him.

The first part of the task is to identify all the services in your local community for each of the subjects in turn. Thus, for Tom you would list all the organisations and facilities available for the elderly in general, and also any that might be needed by Tom for reasons special to him. (You will already have gathered some of this information for Tom as part of an earlier task in Chapter 5.)

The next part of the task is to record whether each of the services you have identified is statutory, non-statutory or private. At the same time, make a note of any special features about the services concerned. Obviously, some people will use many of the same services – Bob and Tom, for example. Don't waste time recording the same material twice!

The final part of the task is to devise a way of setting out the results of your research so that they can be readily understood by a tutor or assessor. This will test a number of your core skills and give you an opportunity to provide evidence of your competence.

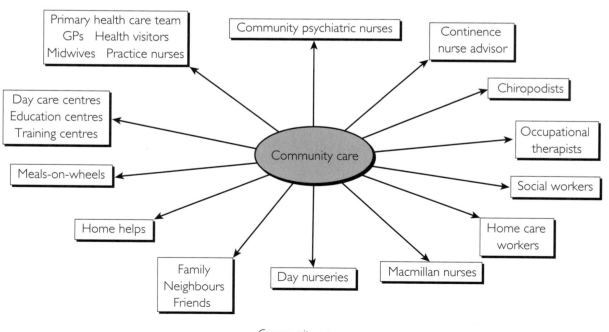

Community care

In particular, it should provide you with an opportunity to practise your information technology skills.∎

RIGHTS AND STANDARDS

Even though some of the original ideals of the welfare state have not survived, we still believe that all citizens have the right to benefit from good standards of public services. This belief is reflected in the recent introduction of a series of Parliamentary Charters with the aim of ensuring that we, the citizens, know what services we are entitled to and what we can expect from these services. The first of these was the **Citizens' Charter**, introduced in 1990.

Each charter aims not just to provide information about the services offered, but to set standards of performance for those providing the services. Two of the charters are of particular interest to us: the **Patients' Charter** (1992) and the **Parents' Charter** (1991). Each has been updated by Parliament since its original publication, so make sure you look at the latest edition.

The Patients' Charter

The January 1995 edition of the Patients' Charter, launched by the Secretary of State for Health, develops rather than alters the principal aims of the original charter. Get a copy from your local library, Citizens' Advice Bureau (CAB), health centre or hospital. Read it through carefully and make sure that you can answer the questions set out below.

 TASK *The Patients' Charter*

1 Do patients have access to their health records?
2 Once you have been placed on a hospital waiting list, what is the maximum time you should wait before admission?
3 How does an individual go about getting a second opinion on his or her condition?
4 Can patients choose whether they want to take part in medical research or medical student training?
5 Do you have to be registered with a general practitioner (GP) in order to receive hospital treatment?
6 To whom would you direct your letter if you wished to make a complaint about the NHS?∎

Raising standards

The charters also aim to improve the standards and quality of the services provided. In the case of the NHS this is a responsibility given to each Regional Health Authority (RHA), which is expected to provide and deliver the highest quality of health care. The RHA must find out whether local people are satisfied with the service they receive. The emphasis is on patient satisfaction:

* Are the waiting times for operations satisfactory?
* Are the waiting times in out-patients' departments satisfactory?
* Are the services provided of satisfactory quality?
* Are the quality and the range of available information satisfactory?

How people respond to these questions will depend on the treatment they receive. But this is not just a matter of their medical treatment: it will also reflect the care they are shown as individuals. People who are attending hospital for treatment, or who are waiting to be admitted, are usually nervous and unsure about the procedures involved. This should be recognised by those providing care, and the needs of the patient should be met in a sensitive and understanding manner. Each individual patient should feel special and secure in the knowledge that all those engaged in their care, from the receptionist at the enquiry desk to the consultant surgeon or physician, understand and know why they are there and what is best for them. Raising standards depends on everyone's contribution – including yours.

Community care

You will have seen that one of the sections in the Patients' Charter deals with **community services**. The professional workers referred to in this section are key members of the community care team: nurses, health visitors and midwives. The standards expected of them are the same as those expected of all professionals working in community care. In the future these standards are likely to set out in local community charters.

The Parents' Charter

The Parents' Charter is primarily concerned with parents' rights in relation to their children's education. In particular it is about each child's right to a good education. Get a copy of the charter and look at the section on special educational needs which relates to children such as Jane.

The Children Act 1989

Schools are legally required to protect the children in their care, as part of the **Education Act 1988**. This legislation was incorporated into the **Children Act 1989**, which laid down strict guidelines about the school's role in linking with other child protection agencies, notably the social services. (You will remember that this was mentioned earlier in connection with child abuse and the local authority child protection register.)

Make sure that you are familiar with this Act. It contains a lot of information about children's rights, and it also provides important information about the procedures and responsibilities of the various agencies involved, including the local authorities. Note how the Act also upholds the central role of the family in using the phrase **parental responsibility** to describe the duties of parents in relation to the care, upbringing and protection of their children. The Act reflects the basic principle that underpins the whole of community care – personal responsibility.

HEALTH PROMOTION

Prevention is better than cure

We have already remarked upon the enormous costs of the NHS and the increasing demands that will continue to be placed on it. The assumption, when the NHS was first established, that once the sick were cured all that would be necessary was to keep people in good health, has proved to be a dream that has never come true. As we've seen, one answer has been to reorganise the NHS in order to increase its efficiency. Another has been to give serious thought to the longer-term goal of preventing illness, and so reducing the demands on the system – prevention is better than cure. Curing illness takes a lot of time and money, *preventing* illness means promoting continuing good health, which in the long run saves time and money.

The idea of preventing illness by promoting good health is not a new one. We've already touched on several examples of what we call **preventative health care**, such as screening, sight and hearing tests, and vaccinations. These are examples of thinking ahead. In addition to these specific aspects of health care, it is important to work more broadly, promoting positive attitudes towards health. One of the main aims of health promotion is to raise people's awareness of the positive benefits of a healthy personal lifestyle. Because this may mean educating people into different ways of living, it is also referred to as **health education**.

Health promotion is a wide-ranging topic. The following sections cover just three aspects of health promotion. Firstly, they deal with its general aims, the nature of its work and the way it is organised. Secondly, they consider very briefly five key areas of health promotion, those relating to diet, alcohol, drugs, sexually transmitted diseases, and cigarette smoking. Thirdly, they focus on the professional skills and understandings required of a care worker when dealing with health promotion issues.

The Health Education Authority

The Government's interest in health promotion is reflected in the establishment of **The Health Education Authority**, a funded agency responsible for informing the public about the virtues and the dangers of particular lifestyles and health behaviours. In most towns and cities there is a **health promotion unit** or **health education unit**, with staff who work with different sections of the local community to encourage them to make choices that work towards healthier lifestyles.

TASK *Health promotion units*
Visit your local health promotion unit. During the visit, find answers to the following questions.

- How many people work in the unit?
- How is the unit funded?
- What does the job of a health promotion officer involve?
- What sort of career backgrounds do the health promotion officers have?
- What does the unit spend its money on?
- Is there a particular health campaign taking place or about take place?
- Is there a charge for materials loaned from the unit?∎

Factors affecting health

Your visit to the unit will have alerted you to the fact that there are no easy answers when the questions relate to people's personal lifestyles and the way these affect their health. It has become clear from health-related research that certain groups and people in the population are more likely to be ill than others, and that these differences are the result of a wide range of different factors.

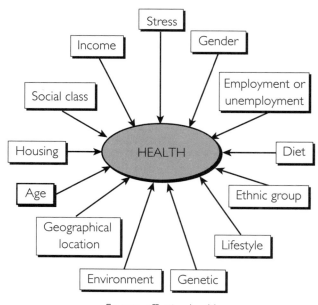

Factors affecting health

Some of these are identified in the diagram on page 86. As you look through them, note that some relate directly to the work you have covered in the GNVQ units. Social, cultural, economic and geographical factors in people's well-being, for example, are covered in Unit 2, Element 2.3. Factors relating to gender, ethnic group, age, and discrimination in general are covered in Unit 4, Element 4.2.

The personal lives of some of the people in Hotspur Street also reflect a number of health factors. Dave's health was affected by his unemployment, Jenny's by the stress caused by Dave's problems. As a family their choice of diet was affected by their restricted budget. Similarly, Bob's health was probably affected by his habit of smoking.

Health promotion campaigns

Health campaigns play an important part in the work of the health promotion units. Look at the list of health messages below. Unlike many of the factors identified above, these are all behaviours over which we as individuals have some control. Because this is so, and because the choices we make in relation to these behaviours can be changed or modified, these are key targets in many health education campaigns.

- Don't eat unhealthy food.
- Don't smoke tobacco.
- Don't drink too much alcohol.
- Don't forget to take plenty of exercise.
- Don't use drugs.
- Don't have unsafe sex.
- Don't forget to look after your teeth and gums.
- Don't forget to carry out breast or testicular self-examination.
- Don't get overweight or underweight.
- Don't get stressed.
- Don't leave your child unvaccinated.

Getting the message across

What effect did the word 'don't' have on you as you read the list? On the receiving end of such advice, how you feel will be an important factor in choosing whether or not to take any notice of it. Sadly, many of the messages linked to health promotion appear to have a finger-wagging style: 'No! Don't do it!' This has come about because many health campaigns are in competition with other campaigns, mainly campaigns by commercial advertisers trying to encourage people to adopt habits or behaviours that, though acceptable in moderation, can be harmful in excess.

Health promoters such as doctors, nurses, care workers, teachers and parents often have to compete with the power of media advertising. Advertising campaigns for cars or for washing powders usually have a glamorous, carefree image. The actual product being promoted may not be the only focus of attention, and all sorts of secondary messages may be very prominent. As in the case of certain car advertisements, the person driving the car is often modelling many other behaviours that have nothing to do with the car itself but which influence the passive observer all the same. 'Secondary advertising' is an interesting and complex topic: you might like to study it yourself when watching advertisements on television.

As a health promoter it is not always easy to overcome the influence of some of the very powerful factors that are affecting people's choices of lifestyle. Imagine the following situation.

Jenny is shopping in a supermarket. Zoë is in the baby seat in the trolley, and Steve and Nick are taking turns to get the food from the shelves to put into the trolley. When they arrive at the sweets section, Steve and Nick ask if they can have a toffee bar called Nine Lives, which has a card game attached to it. They have seen this advertised on television. Jenny does not want to buy Nine Lives: she wants to protect the children's teeth, and the boys have already had sweets that day; she cannot afford Nine Lives, which is more expensive than the sweets they normally have; and she does not want the boys to play with the violent war game that has been advertised as coming free with the bar of Nine Lives. Jenny says 'No', and the boys create a fuss.

The dilemma that Jenny faces is not only a health promotion choice. Primarily, she wanted to protect the boys' teeth, but there are financial and moral issues to be considered too. If Steve and Nick have seen the advertisement – and that is what that attracted them to the Nine Lives toffee bar – this probably means that the advertisement was screened during a children's programme. Television, newspapers, magazines and the cinema inform us about what is going on in the world and expose us to trends and behaviours that may be beyond our own experience. Much of the advertising information that we are exposed to is to do with products that may have an influence on our health. Advertising has a powerful and influential effect on what we do and how we do it, and is often targeted towards specific age groups of viewers such as Nick and Steve.

Eating for pleasure or eating to live?

Food is an important part of our lives and the term **healthy eating** plays a prominent part in the work of health promotion. You probably already know something about the different types of foods that we eat and their use in the body, but many of the people you will be caring for in the future will not. How healthy is *your* diet?

▶ TASK Diet

Make a list of all the different items of food you ate, from when you got up yesterday morning until you went to bed at night. Include all meals, and any food eaten in between meals.

Then find a book in the library on food and nutrition, and identify which foods are classed as:

- carbohydrate;
- protein;
- fat.

Note why we need a certain amount of each nutrient, and also which minerals and vitamins we require and how much water we should drink. This is what we know as a **balanced diet**.

Finally, return to the list of food you consumed yesterday, and compare it with the types and quantities of food reflected in a balanced diet. Is your diet a healthy one?∎

LIFESTYLE CHANGES

Getting people to understand what is meant by a healthy lifestyle is one thing; influencing them so that they want to change their ways is another.

Let us imagine that Bob has returned home and is making a confident recovery. He can dress himself with a little help from Cath; he can use the toilet independently, and he has only a slight slurring of his speech. He has worked hard with the professionals who have helped in his rehabilitation, but his blood pressure is still too high, which might increase the risk of further strokes. Unfortunately, Bob has not been able to give up his addiction to smoking cigarettes, and since his discharge from hospital he has put on weight because he insists on eating chips with everything followed by cream cakes.

While you must respect Bob's choice of food, you may find yourself in the position of having to support Cath in persuading Bob to eat food that will help his recovery and reduce his weight. This situation could lead to a difficult dilemma for you. How do you support the carer and the patient at the same time? You know Bob should be eating plenty of vegetables, salads, white fish and lean meats, and drinking plenty of fluids: when he does, however, he gets depressed and is rude and critical of Cath. When she presents him with a salad he is angry with her for not giving him the stodgy, fatty foods, high in carbohydrates, that he likes.

The way in which clients and patients react in such situations often reflects the fears they have about their condition. This in turn may test your patience and sensitivity. As a care worker you cannot choose to act on the basis that you like some clients more than others: you must treat *everyone* without prejudice. Disliking people within a professional context is something you must learn to deal with. Since it is the client who is always at the centre of any debate on health and social care, you as care worker must see each person in an objective way, while being understanding in difficult situations.

Health promotion: sexually transmitted diseases

Sexually transmitted diseases (**STDs**) are usually passed on through sexual intercourse and you will have heard of some of them: they include syphilis, genital herpes, gonorrhoea, and occasionally candidiasis.

Most STDs can be treated successfully, but not all: the **human immunodeficiency virus** (**HIV**) which causes the **acquired immune deficiency syndrome** (**AIDS**), cannot be cured. During the 1980s and 1990s there have been many vigorous health campaigns to raise awareness about the risk of contracting this infection. Health promotion campaigns focused on reducing the spread of HIV and AIDS by encouraging people:

- to have safe sex, by using condoms;
- to limit the number of sexual partners;
- not to share hypodermic needles.

The virus is passed through infected body fluids; a number of people in Britain have become infected through receiving contaminated blood transfusions. At present we still know very little about HIV infection, but because it is so serious and life-threatening it is an issue that you will become more and more aware of as you prepare to join the workforce in the health care sector.

Health promotion: alcohol, drugs and solvents

Drinks such as beer, spirits and wine contain different amounts of **alcohol**, just as different **drugs** come in various strengths. The main difference between alcohol and drug addiction is that alcohol consumption is generally considered to be socially acceptable, so that alcohol can easily be bought provided that you are over 18 years of age, whereas drugs such as cannabis, cocaine and heroin are not widely seen as acceptable and are illegal and not publicly available. Sniffing **solvents** – substances such as petrol, glue and lighter fuels – can also be addictive.

The misuse of alcohol, and drug and substance abuse, can eventually lead to death. Long before this happens, however, much social, family and personal misery will be caused. Alcohol, drug and solvent abuse are all potentially dangerous: you need to be aware of the way people behave when they are using such stimulants.

Health promotion: smoking tobacco

This particular 'don't' exemplifies some of the key practical skills required by the care worker when dealing with health promotion issues. For many people, young and old, cigarette smoking is a key factor in influencing their health. In Bob's case it is likely that it has contributed to his present medical condition. Health campaigns informing people of the dangers of smoking have a high priority in health promotion and education programmes.

TASK *Giving up smoking (1)*

Collect together as much health promotion information as you can on smoking tobacco. You will find that different materials target different sections of the community and are written in a style appropriate to that group. Groups will include:

- children who have not yet started to smoke;
- young people who are smokers but not long-term addicts;
- older people who want to stop smoking.

Sort through your material and divide it between the three groups above, noting how and why it is appropriate for the chosen target group.

Bob would be a typical target for the literature related to the older group. However, getting Bob to realise the harm that smoking is doing to his health is not likely to be easy.∎

TASK *Giving up smoking (2)*

It is your responsibility to approach Bob with the information you have obtained on smoking, and to suggest to him that he should think about giving up the habit.

His first response is this: 'I've been smoking since I was a soldier in the Second World War, over fifty years ago. I couldn't stop smoking now if I wanted to. Anyway, what good would it do?'

Find a partner in your group. One of you should take the part of Bob, the other the part of the care worker trying to encourage Bob to give up smoking. Begin by looking carefully through the literature so that you know exactly why smoking is a particular danger for Bob. The person playing the part of Bob must start with the response above, but after that can reply as he or she wishes in the light of the advice and encouragement given by the care worker.

Now reverse roles, and then compare what you have learned from the exercise, as a care worker and as Bob.∎

Making decisions

As you may have discovered, there are a number of do's and don'ts involved in trying to help people to change their behaviours. We've already noted that most of us aren't impressed when people wag their fingers at us and treat us like naughty children. Patience and sensitivity are virtues, as are encouragement and sympathy. In helping Bob to give up smoking, for example, showing that you understand how difficult a decision it is for him is important; even more important will be a positive commitment to help Bob achieve his goal, as opposed to merely telling him what he needs to do and then leaving him to it.

In your literature you may have found that there are a number of ways of helping Bob to give up smoking. Reward systems, for example, are sometimes used as a means of encouraging smokers to reduce gradually the number of cigarettes they smoke. It may help to keep a diary to record such things as:

- Where did you smoke the cigarette?
- What was the time?
- Were you alone or with others?
- If you were with others, did they smoke a cigarette too?
- Were you craving for a smoke? Place this on a rating of 1–5: 1 = low craving; 5 = high craving.
- How did you feel after you had smoked the cigarette?

Bob needs to know about such methods, and that you will support him through this difficult period. He also needs to know that he may be able to receive positive support through group therapy sessions in which long-term and short-term benefits can be identified. Smokers who have been successful in breaking the habit are often present at these sessions to support and encourage the person who is trying to give up smoking. The reformed smoker is well placed to empathise with the person trying to quit. There are also other helpful supports for the long-term smoker, such as nicotine chewing gum or patches, hypnosis, and herbal cigarettes. For people such as Bob it often takes more than one attempt to stop smoking, because of the addictive nature of nicotine.

So much for some of the do's. There is one important don't: don't make personal judgements about people's behaviours. However sad it may be to see the result of careful rehabilitation undone by the actions of the patient or client, it is not for you to voice your opinions about how other people should behave. Your responsibility is to make sure that Bob is fully informed about the consequences of his action, and the ways that it may affect his health in the future. It is then up to Bob to make an informed decision about any changes to his lifestyle.

One further word of warning. In situations such as this, you are likely to be exposed to personal details and information about people's private lives. At all times you must respect the client's privacy and dignity. Treat others as you would wish to be treated yourself.

CARING FOR YOURSELF

There has been a great deal in this book about caring for others. What has gone unsaid is the importance you should place on your own health and well-being. Caring is a stressful occupation: it takes a lot out of you, emotionally and physically. The way you care for your own health and well-being is critical if you are to remain healthy and fit for the job.

Make sure that you have time to relax, and time to socialise with friends who do not place demands on you. Keep up the hobbies and sports that you have enjoyed in the past. Don't take on more than you can manage, and learn to say 'no' when you need to. Try to take the occasional break away, and enjoy a complete change of scenery. Finally, make absolutely sure that you get sufficient sleep.

Remember that you, too, are special.

KEY WORDS AND TECHNICAL TERMS

Beveridge Report A report by Sir William Beveridge, published in 1942. It surveyed the social, economic and educational conditions in Britain at the time of

You too are special!

the Second World War. It was this report which, over the following few years, provided the basis for the legislation that was to establish the welfare state.

Budget-holding GPs General practitioners who hold and manage their own budgets. How they spend their money on the patients in their care is a matter for their own judgement.

Children Act 1989 An Act of Parliament identifying children's rights to protection, and the procedures and responsibilities of the organisations and agencies involved in ensuring this protection.

Parents' Charter (1994) Part of the Citizens' Charter: it sets out the rights of parents in terms of their children's education, and the standards to be expected of the education service.

Patients' Charter (1995) Part of the Citizens' Charter: it sets out the standards of service to be expected of the NHS, and the rights of patients in relation to these services.

Preventative health care An approach to health care based on the belief that preventing ill health is as important as concentrating on curing people once they are ill. It is also a way of saving money. For example, warning cigarette smokers about the dangers to their health is a form of preventative health care: it seeks to stop them from becoming ill.

Private services Health and care services provided by privately run organisations, usually for profit.

Statutory services Health and care services provided by the government through the Department of Health.

Trust hospitals Hospitals that hold and manage their own budgets independently of the Regional and District Health Authorities.

Voluntary services Health and care services provided by charitable organisations, though some of them also receive financial support from the State.

Welfare state This was established by 1948 through a series of Acts of Parliament, which set out to provide every citizen with the right to a job, good housing, a free education, and free health and care services.

8 • Sources of information and help

This chapter gives an overview of sources of information and help you may find useful. In this chapter you will:

- be given information about some of the key publications relating to health and social care and a booklist of further reading for the course;
- be made aware of some of the main services provided by libraries;
- be provided with a bank of names and addresses of organisations and agencies that may be useful to you in your professional role as a care worker.

In Chapter 1 you were given some general advice and guidance on how to get the best out of your studies. You were also introduced to the idea of taking responsibility for your own learning, which means knowing what facilities and resources are available to you in your college or school, and knowing how to use them effectively. This chapter identifies some of the main sources of information and help available to you.

LIBRARIES

Libraries provide much more than books. They also hold a variety of publications on specialist topics which you may need to refer to when carrying out assignments, particularly in the later stages of your course when you will be expected to read more widely and in greater depth. Such publications include the following.

Government publications

Reports These are particularly useful because they set out very clearly the thinking and recommendations behind the issues under review. Of particular value are government reports, which often provide the basis for subsequent parliamentary legislation. Thus, to understand the thinking behind the NHS and Community Care Act 1990 you need to look at the Griffiths' Report of 1988, upon which it was based.

White Papers These are also useful because they provide a statement about future government legislation on major policy issues. You will find, for example, that there was a White Paper on 'The Development of Community Care', which was published in 1963! It took 27 years for the White Paper to be acted on.

Acts of Parliament Copies of Acts of Parliament are published by the government's publishers (Her Majesty's Stationery Office, HMSO) and kept in the larger libraries. These can be helpful when you want to know exactly what an Act such as the Children Act 1989 says, rather than rely on what someone else has written about it.

Bulletins and surveys These are particularly useful: they provide statistical data relating to a whole variety of social and economic issues. The one you are likely to find most useful is *Social Trends*, which provides data on such topics as unemployment, expenditure, poverty, welfare, and homelessness. This is a government publication (HMSO) and is produced by the **Office of Population Censuses and Surveys** (**OPCS**), which also publishes, on a five-yearly basis, statistical data of its own – for example, on family income patterns.

Other publications

Newspapers Libraries are likely to take both national and local newspapers. Certain newspapers, notably the *Guardian* and the *Independent*, carry feature articles on health and care topics on particular days of the week. Make a note of these. Your library may keep back copies of these newspapers.

Encyclopaedias and dictionaries These are helpful in emergencies when you find that you need information about a word or area of knowledge with which you are unfamiliar. Remember that these will only provide you with a general definition and outline of what you need to know, and they will use material that may quickly become outdated. Use them only as a starting-point for further research.

Journals and periodicals These are dealt with separately below.

All of the above publications are likely to be part of the library's **reference collection**. This means that they cannot be taken out on loan, but must be used in the library. In certain cases the library may not hold the book or document that you want to use, but they may well be able to obtain it for you through an **inter-library loan**, by borrowing it for you from another library for a short period. This can take a week or more, so you need to plan your work carefully in advance and try to anticipate what you will need rather than leave everything to the last minute. Remember the advice in Chapter 1 about the need to manage your own time effectively.

One further piece of advice: it's easy to read articles in newspapers, periodicals and journals, and think that you will remember where you read each article. In practice you may forget, so always make a careful note of the title, the date and the page number of the item you have been consulting, as well as the name of the publication. Get used to doing this as a matter of habit, then when you come to providing the bibliography for your assignment you won't waste time trying to find the information that you need. If you decide that the best way of keeping track of the things you read is to make photocopies of them, make sure that you don't break the law. Find out about **copyright laws**, which you must observe.

Your library is likely to possess other facilities and resources and these will be made known to you as part of your induction to the school or college. The library will certainly have computerised information and resource services such as Prestel or Teletext, and probably CD-ROM. These may be part of a resource base within the library specially equipped to help you with the more practical aspects of your learning.

Resources will include computers that are available to you outside class time for practising your keyboard skills, for word-processing your assignments and for making use of the software available for developing your own specialist knowledge. There may also be a wide range of materials and facilities useful to you when putting together and presenting your

assignments, such as collections of audio-visual materials, reprographic equipment, cameras, and video and tape recorders. Some resource bases may offer you the chance to try your hand at desk-top publishing.

The people and resources are on hand to help you make the best of the opportunities presented to you. In the end, however, it's up to you to make the most of them: that's what taking responsibility for your own learning means. Don't be afraid to ask when you need advice or help.

Journals and periodicals

Reference has already been made to the specialist journals and periodicals covering a variety of topics and issues in health and social care, which you need to be aware of at the beginning of your course. Your tutors will encourage you to refer to such publications where they contain articles of particular relevance to your studies. You should also get used to using some of your free time to keep up to date with the issues that are being discussed in the professional journals and periodicals relating to health and care.

It's worth keeping a file of relevant articles and news cuttings that may be of use to you. For instance, an article on the future of community care or new discoveries about the causes of Alzheimer's disease is going to be relevant to an assignment at some stage. The following list identifies some of the main journals and periodicals relating to health and social care.

British Journal of Social Work Published once every two months, this contains a wide variety of articles relevant to social work.

Resource base

Library

Care Weekly A news magazine published weekly for social work and care professionals.

Community Care Published weekly, this investigates and reports on community care, reviews books, and advertises courses and jobs in social work and community care.

Health Education News Published six times a year by the Health Education Authority, this provides information about health risks and health promotion.

Nursing Times Published weekly, this deals with all aspects of health and advertises courses, seminars and jobs.

Social Studies Review (1985–1991), now **Sociology Review** (1991–) Published four times a year (September, November, February and April), this examines a variety of sociological issues.

Social Trends Published annually, and referred to above.

Social Work Today Published weekly, this deals with broad issues in social work and in social services; it also advertises jobs in social care.

SELF-HELP

It's easy to overlook the most immediate source of help available to you: yourself and your colleagues. As a member of a group, you have an excellent resource in the expertise and experience of the people in it. You can help yourself and each other in all sorts of ways. For instance:

- Television programmes that are relevant to your course can be identified, watched as a group and discussed. Documentaries on most television channels deal frequently with topical issues of relevance to your course. If you know of these in advance, they can be recorded and watched later.
- Radio programmes also cover topical issues that can help you to keep up to date and acquire useful information. Look at the programmes advertised and, if something looks interesting, arrange for one person to listen to it and tape it for the rest of the group to listen to later.
- Arrangements can be made for each person in the group to subscribe to or look at a particular journal, and to identify useful articles for the rest of the group.

LOCAL ORGANISATIONS AND AGENCIES

Many local sources of information are worth knowing about – they could be of use to you when researching a particular area of health and care. Remember, however, that people who work in these organisations are busy people and there are procedures to follow when making contact. You may be in a rush and want the information from the agency quickly, but their priorities may be very different to yours. Remember the importance of forward planning. If you are writing away for information, enclose a self-addressed envelope and expect to wait for at least ten days before you receive anything back. If the whole group requires the same information, write collectively – the agency won't welcome twenty-five requests for the same thing. You should be able to arrange between yourselves to share or copy the information.

If you wish to visit an agency, make contact first by writing or telephoning, and ask for an appointment. Indicate clearly what it is you want to discuss. When you do finally meet the person concerned, make sure that you are well prepared and clear about what it is you need to know so as not to waste his or her time. If you are hoping to tape-record the discussion or interview, or to take photographs, make sure you get permission first. It is also important that you acknowledge the contribution made by the agency or individual. A few moments to express your appreciation are worthwhile, and may help other students subsequently when they ask for help.

Local contacts

Local contacts are especially useful. Try to get to know what sources of advice and information are available locally. Depending on where you live, some or all of the specialist contacts listed below may be available. In earlier chapters in the book you were asked to locate many of them; make sure by the time you have finished the book that you have located them all, and any others that have been brought to your attention.

- Age Concern
- Citizens' Advice Bureau
- General hospital with accident and emergency department
- Gingerbread
- Health promotion unit
- Library
- Local education authority
- Local authority social services department
- Relate
- Samaritans
- Volunteer bureau

USEFUL ADDRESSES

It is also important for you to be aware of agencies that are nationally rather than locally based. The following list provides a selection.

Action for Research into Multiple Sclerosis (ARMS) 4a Chapel Hill, Stanstead, Essex CM24 8AG.

Action on Smoking and Health (ASH) 109 Gloucester Place, London W1H 4DH.

Action through Allergy (AAA) 23–24 George Street, Richmond, Surrey TW9 1JY.

Advisory Committee for the Education of Romany and other Travellers (ACERT) Mott House, Bestow, Harlow, Essex CM20 3AG.

Afro-Caribbean Education Resource Centre Wyvil Road, London SW8 2TJ.

Age Concern England Astral House, 1268 London Road, London SW16 4ER.

Alcoholics Anonymous (AA) General Service Office, PO Box 1, Stonebow House, Stonebow, York YO1 2NJ.

Alzheimer's Disease Society 158–160 Balham High Road, London SW12 9BN.

Association for Post-Natal Illness 7 Gowan Avenue, London SW6 6RH.

Association of 'Crossroads' Care Attendants Ltd 10 Regent Place, Rugby CV21 2PN.

Barnardo's Tanners Lane, Barkingside, Ilford, Essex IG6 1QC.

Body Positive 51B Philbeech Gardens, London SW5 9EB.

British Heart Foundation 14 Fitzhardinge Street, London W1H 4DH.

Cancer Relief Anchor House, 15–19 Britten Street, London SW3 3TZ.

Carers National Association 20–25 Glasshouse Yard, London EC1A 4JS.

Central Council for Education and Training in Social Work (CCETSW) Information Service (England), Derbyshire House, St Chad's Street, London WC1H 8AD.

Centrepoint Soho 5th Floor, 14a Gloucester Mansions, Cambridge Circus, London WC2H 8HD.

Childline 50 Studd Street, London NW1 0QY.

Child Poverty Action Group (CPAG) 1–5 Bath Street, London EC1V 9PY.

Commission for Racial Equality (CRE) Elliot House, 10–12 Allington Street, London SW1E 5EH.

Cruse Bereavement Care 126 Sheen Road, Richmond, Surrey TW9 1UR.

Disabled Living Foundation (DLF) 380–384 Harrow Road, London W9 2HU.

Down's Syndrome Association 153–155 Mitcham Road, London SW17 9PG.

Eating Disorders Association Sackville Place, 44 Magdalen Street, Norwich NR3 1JE.

Equal Opportunities Commission Overseas House, Quay Street, Manchester M3 3HN.

European Community Information Office 8 Storeys Gate, London SW1P 3AT.

Family Rights Group The Print House, 18 Ashwin Street, London E8 3DL.

Gingerbread 35 Wellington Street, London WC2E 7BN.

Health Education Authority Hamilton House, Mableton Place, London WC1H 9TX.

Health Service Careers PO Box 204, London SE5 7ES.

Health Visitors' Association 50 Southwark Street, London SE1 1UN.

Help the Aged 16–18 St James's Walk, London EC1R 0BE.

Incest Survivors in Strength (ISIS) 23 Tunstall Road, London SW9 8BS.

Kids' Clubs Network Bellerive House, 3 Muirfield Crescent, London E14 9SZ.

MENCAP (Royal Society for Mentally Handicapped Children and Adults) 22 Harley Street, London EC1Y 0RT.

MIND (National Association for Mental Health) 15–19 Broadway, London E15 4BQ.

National Association of Citizens' Advice Bureaux Myddelton House, 115–123 Pentonville Road, London N1 9LZ.

National Childminding Association 8 Masons Hill, Bromley, Kent BR2 9EY.

National Children's Bureau 8 Wakley Street, London EC1V 7QE.

National Council for Voluntary Organisations (NCVO) Regent's Wharf, 8 All Saints Street, London N1 9RL.

National Society for the Prevention of Cruelty to Children (NSPCC) 67 Saffron Hill, London EC1N 8RS.

Positively Women 333 Gray's Inn Road, London WC1X 8PX.

Pregnancy Advisory Service 13 Charlotte Street, London W1P 1HD.

Relate National Marriage Guidance Herbert Gray College, Little Church Street, Rugby CV21 3AP.

Release 169 Commercial Street, London E1 6BW.

Samaritans 10 The Grove, Slough SL1 1QP.

Shelter 88 Old Street, London EC1V 9HU.

Terrence Higgins Trust 52–54 Gray's Inn Road, London WC1X 6LT.

Women's Health 52 Featherstone Street, London EC1Y 8RT.

Women's Health Concern PO Box 1629, London W8 6AU.

Women's National Cancer Control Campaign 128 Curtain Road, London EC2A 3AR.

WRVS (Women's Royal Voluntary Service) 234–244 Stockwell Road, London SW9 9SP.

The title of the group or agency will give you a good idea of the work and activity it's engaged in. Those that are less clear, such as Positively Women (a group for women who are HIV-positive) and Centrepoint (an organisation to assist the homeless), may need some investigation before contact is made. Your tutors will be able to clarify the roles of the groups you are unsure about. Alternatively, ask in the library for the directories which identify all the voluntary agencies in existence in the UK.

SUGGESTED FURTHER READING

Allen, N. *Making Sense of the Children Act* (Longmans, 1993).

Baldwin, D. *All About Children* (Oxford University Press, 1983).

Ewles, L. and Simnett, I. *Promoting Health: A practical guide to health education* (Wiley, 1985).

Hayes, N. *Principles of Social Psychology*, Chapter 1 (Lawrence Erlbaum Associates, 1993).

Lindon, J. and L. *Caring for the Under-8s: Working to achieve good practice* (Macmillan Press, 1993).

Lindon, J. and L. *Caring for Young Children: A workbook for early years workers* (Macmillan Press, 1994).

Moore, S. *Social Welfare Alive!* (Stanley Thornes, 1993).

Northledge, A. *The Good Study Guide* (Open University Press, 1990).

St. John Ambulance, British Red Cross and St. Andrew's Ambulance Association. *First Aid Manual* (Dorling Kindersley, 1994).

Sillars, S. *Caring for People: A workbook for care workers* (Macmillan Press, 1992).

Smyth, T. *Caring for Older People: Creating approaches to good practice* (Macmillan Press, 1992).

Windmill, V. *Ageing Today* (Edward Arnold, 1990).

Windmill, V. *Caring for the Elderly* (Pitman)

Williams, *A Practical Approach to Caring* (Pitman)

Young, P. *Mastering Social Welfare*, 3rd edn (Macmillan Press, 1995).

Index